CONCEPTS IN COMMUNICATION INFORMATICS & LIBRARIANSHIP (CICIL)

For a list of titles in this series, see pp. 190-92 at the end of the book

Concepts in Communication
Informatics & Librarianship-35

General Editor: **S.P. Agrawal**

PROBLEMS OF COLLECTION DEVELOPMENT IN SPECIAL LIBRARIES

M.S. SRIDHAR
Head, Library and Documentation ISRO Satellite Centre
Bangalore

CONCEPT PUBLISHING COMPANY, NEW DELHI 110059

ISBN 81-7022-428-4

First Published 1992

Published and Printed by
Ashok Kumar Mittal
Concept Publishing Company
A/15-16, Commercial Block, Mohan Garden
NEW DELHI 110059 (India)

Lasertypeset by
Microtech Advance Printing Systems (Pvt.) Ltd.
H-13, Bali Nagar
NEW DELHI 110015

DEDICATED TO

My sister late Smt. Gowramma

who nourished me like her son

GENERAL EDITOR'S INTRODUCTION

Special libraries are established to serve the needs of clienteles with specialised interests – the scientists, the planners, the lawyers, the industrialists, the economists, the bankers etc., unlike associated with the sponsoring organisations/enterprises in realisation of their goals and purposes. Unlike other academic libraries (University libraries for example) therefore, special libraries collection is generally limited to a single subject or a group of subjects which are interrelated.

Whatever the type of a library, Collection Development (CD) is the most important job of a librarian. In order to build up effective collection it is necessary that a librarian should have a good understanding of the basic facts about the subject interests of the library, as also a thorough knowledge about the methods of book selection, book procurement and the book trade. The Librarian should also be able to assess the present needs of the users of the library and to forsee their future requirements. In a public library the acquisition of the library materials, which generally include books on fiction and those on popular non-fiction, does not pose a problem. However, this cannot be said of a university library which has to provide all type of materials in all the subject fields for its students, teaching staff and researchers at the levels. For this very reason the collection development in a university library is a difficult and challenging task for the university librarian. For a librarian of a specialised library this job becomes even more exacting, ardous and complex in view of the fact that every possible type of material within the scope of a very wide stretch of specialisation of the library and that too in depth is required to be acquired. In a special library, the emphasis being on the current information, the focus is normally less on published monographs generally brought out late in the evenings and more on periodicals (which report latest in the news) and other type of literature like abstracts, indexes, translations, reports and proceedings of conferences and seminars, etc., of government departments, learned societies and academics, patents, specifications, and non-book materials such as micro-forms, maps, charts, slides, films, floppies and photographs, etc. including gray literature. Acquisition of these materials, which are ordinarily not available through normal commercial channels, makes heavy demands on the time, energy and capabilities of the senior staff of a special library. Particularly uphill – rather exasperating – is the task to obtain publications of government departments due to cumbersome bureaucratic procedure not unmixed with indifferent attitude of the government staff concerned. Furthermore, since the main purpose of the special library is to further the interests of the sponsoring organisation, the librarian is expected to be fully informed not only all of the projects and programmes of the organisation, but also of the interests, qualifications and capabilities of its members of staff so as to meet the requirements meaningfully.

Literature search on CD in libraries general is not difficult. The literature with regard to the holdings of special or technical libraries however is not much. Fewer are the books or reports on the subject in the context of Indian scenario. The present volume fulfils this need of the special libraries in India giving a detailed and incisive examination of the problems which a librarian of a special library has to face in connection with selection and procurement of the documents for the library. The special feature of the book is citation of CD case studies which elucidate and highlight the problems and self suggest their possible solution.

S.P. AGRAWAL

FOREWORD

In this age of information explosion, librarians all over the world, more particularly in developing countries like India, are facing a number of problems in developing a dynamic and a usable collection of information resources oriented to user needs. There are a number of documents on the selection and acquisition of documents in a Library. Most of these are theoretical in nature. Further, special libraries have their own typical problems, more so in India. The author in this monograph presents specific problems in collection development in special libraries based on his rich experience at the Indian Space Research Organisation, Bangalore (India).

To build a rich, live and a comprehensive collection, it is essential for a librarian to know, assess, and forecast user requirements. Hence, the document opens with demand forecasting methods and assessment of information requirements of users. Obviously, these issues need active user participation and in Chapter 3 the author deals with various issues relating to user participation in collection development. He narrates in detail reasons for low user participation and offers suggestions thereof.

In Chapter 4, the author considers the problems of selection and acquisition of documents. As many as 22 types of problems have been identified and explained. All these are live problems, which a librarian faces in his daily work.

Book procurement delay is a nagging problem in the Indian context. Special attention has been given to this in Chapter 5.

Technical Reports which constitute a significant part of special library collection pose their own problems which the author analyses in depth in the Chapter 6.

Microforms literature is steadily gaining ground in special libraries. As against the printed documents, microforms collection development has its own typical problems which are described at length in Chapter 7. The next one (Chapter 8) takes the reader to issues relating to Standing Order, Dealer Library Plan, etc.

The last set of problems (Chapter 9) deal with journal subscription which is another oft-demanded literature in special libraries.

In bringing home all these problems, Dr. Sridhar has adopted a style which could be characterised as lucid, direct and simple to understand. The case studies introduced appropriately enhance the value of the work.

The document, thus, fills a gap in [illegible]ary literature relating to collection development. It is a significant contribution which could be used with profit by both special librarians and teachers in Library and Information Science.

DR. H.A. KHAN
Professor, Department of Library & Information Science, University of Mysore, Mysore

PREFACE

This is my second book in librarianship. Sometime ago a well-wisher suggested me to concentrate more on state-of-the-art areas like computerisation, networking and other latest information technology aspects of librarianship than user-research, collection development, collection management and evaluation and the like. I tried to convince him in vain of importance of these most fundamental and basic areas of librarianship. I have more than one reason to choose such subjects for my papers and books. Academic work in general and research in particular in this profession has always been taking an upper hand in deciding the fore-front areas of librarianship and what they pursue are considered to be the important areas in the profession. I am aware of the views of academicians on a research work or a book or an article which is neither in the so-called state-of-the-art and fore-front areas nor fitting into the syllabi of library schools. Yet I strongly feel that integration of problems faced by practitioners with research and academic works in the profession is the need of the hour. There are a number of books on collection development in libraries. But only a few highlight practical problems with illustrative case studies. Collection development is the most discussed, the least understood and practiced area of librarianship.

This book is essentially a compendium of over a dozen papers published by me during the past eight years or so. I have thoroughly edited them to fit into a logical sequence, to eliminate obsolete information and to add gaps in the contents. I have also added an introduction, a conclusion and a chapter on problems of journal subscription afresh to make the contents of the book fairly complete. Repetition of issues and problems are minimised. I have concentrated mainly on practical problems in special libraries with case studies embedded wherever necessary. Yet I cannot dare to claim anywhere near exhaustive or comprehensive coverage of vast area like collection development.

I am highly grateful to Concept Publishing Company for publishing the book and to Dr.H.A. Khan for providing a foreword to the book.

M.S. SRIDHAR

CONTENTS

LIST OF TABLES

GOC	Good Offices Committee (India)
GRA&I	Government Reports Announcements and Index
GSFC	Goddard Space Flight Centre (NASA)
HMSO	Her Majesty's Stationery Office (UK)
HIP	High Information Potential
IASLIC	Indian Association of Special Libraries & Information Centre
ICR	Institute for Communication Research (Stanford University)
IEE	Institution of Electrical Engineers (UK)
IEEE	Institute of Electrical & Electronics Engineers (USA)
IEG	Information Exchange Group (NIH Project)
IMC	International Micrographics Congress
IME	Institution of Mechanical Engineers
INFROSS	Information Requirements of the Social Sciences
ISAC	ISRO Satellite Centre (India)
ISRO	Indian Space Research Organisation
ISRG	Information Systems Research Group (USA)
ISB	Information Seeking Behaviour
ISI	Indian Standards Institution
ISR	Institute for Social Research (University of Michigan)
ISRG	Information Systems Research Group (USA)
IST	Indian Space Technologists
JHU	Johns Hopkins University
JPL	Jet Propulsion Laboratory (USA)
JPRS	Joint Publications Research Service (USA)
LC	Library of Congress (USA)
LIP	Low Information Potential
LSTSR	Limited Scientific and Technical Aerospace Reports
M	Monthly
MAGB	Microfilm Association of Great Britain
MEDLARS	Medical Literature Analysis and Retrieval System
MIL	US Military Standards (USA)
MIT	Massachusetts Institute of Technology
NACA	National Advisory Committee for Aeronautics (Now NASA, USA)

NASA	National Aeronautics and Space Administration (USA)
NASDA	National Space Development Agency (Japan)
NBS	National Bureau of Standards (USA)
NIH	National Institute of Health (USA)
NISP	National Information System for Psychology (APA Project)
NISPA	National Information System for Physics and Astronomy (AIP Project)
NISSAT	National Information System for Science and Technology (India)
NLL	National Lending Library (Later BLLD)
NMA	National Micrographics Association (USA)
NMI	Not Manufacturred in India
NRCD	National Reprographics Centre for Documentation (now Cimtech)
NSF	National Science Foundation
NTIS	National Technical Information Service (USA)
OGL	Open General Licence
ONERA	Office National d'Etudes et de Recherches Aerospatalere
ORG	Operations Research Group (Case Institute of Technology)
p	Page/s
P	Pound Sterling
PIE	Physics Information Exchange (AIP Project)
PP	Pergamon Press
Q	Quarterly
RAC	Reliability Analysis Centre
RAE	Royal Aeronautical Establishment (UK)
RAM	Random Alarm Mechanism
RDT&E	Research, Development, Test and Evaluation
RP	Reference Publications
SAE	Society of Automotive Engineers
SDR	Solution Development Record
SIAM	Society for Industrial & Applied Mathematics (USA)
SIE	Scientific Information Exchange (APA Project)

video cassettes, photographs, microforms, etc. It may also have large part of internally generated information and classified information.

There are a number of factors which affect collection development in a library. The community or institution or clientele to be served, purposes and objectives of the library, present collection, available financial, human, informational, inspirational, recreational, bibliographical, evaluative and other resources, possibilities of resource sharing, modes of information transactions, current demand and use of information by users, traditions, publishing patterns, alternative to purchases, etc. (Hazen, 1982; Magrill and Hickey, 1984). Ideally library collection is deliberately created and developed and it should not be let to happen or built. "As in music, developing suggests elaboration, or as in chess, developing suggests keeping in mind the many possible uses, or the power of every piece, or every item in the collection (Pankake, 1984, p. 188). In other words, collections are the results of development and not evolution. Each of the item selected to a library collection reflects the interaction of above factors and forces.

Though everyone agrees that a written collection development policy is a must for any library, many libraries do not venture to have a written policy. Once policies are explicitly formulated, they must be written to give orderly expression or articulation of priorities and consistent implementation. If it is just lethargy in some cases, some think it may not be worth the trouble to design a collection development policy manual. A few may even put forth an argument that many libraries have excellent collections without having a policy manual. A collection development policy manual to a library is like a 'documentation' for a software package. It tells the nature and scope of the collection, sets priorities, calls for commitment to organisation goals, provides inclusion and exclusion guides, eliminates personal biases of selector, helps to maintain consistency by orienting new staff and controlling old staff, aids resolving complaints, weeding and evaluation of collection and collection development programme and serves as a public relations and accountability tool (Evans, 1987, p. 66-67). A successful collection development manual describes the users or patrons to be served, parameters of library's holdings or subject boundaries of the collection, bibliographic structure of the field, kinds of programmes supported, budget allocation, limitations governing the selection, priorities, subject areas and formats covered, evaluation of suppliers, responsibility of collection development, languages and geographical areas to be covered, detailed collecting code divided by classification to be placed according to levels of collecting density and intensity, ways of dealing with exchanges, gifts, weeding, censorship and evaluation. It forces one to give consideration to unspoken and unrecorded assumptions, helps think systematically about collection development, reduces the complexity of collection development process and improves the quality of collection development work (Perkins, 1982). 'Guidelines for collection development' issued by Resources and Technical Services Division of ALA is a useful tool in preparing a collection development policy manual.

Collection development and management process starts with understanding and updating the knowledge of requirements of users and anticipating their demands. Then follows the selection and matching of available information resources/products with user requirements and their anticipated as well as current demands. In other words selection of items and the actual process of acquiring reading materials/information sources itself is a wide area of professional work. Systematic, reliable and continuous collection evaluation and management is equally important in getting appropriate feedback for collection development process and also to identify obsolete, irrelevant and unused part of collection in order to decide on remote/compact storage and/or discarding. Collection development is not an end in itself. Nor reading materials are selected and acquired to balance the growth of collection but to meet information requirements of users. Periodic reporting of accomplishments of collection development activity would help collection management to a great extent.

Collection development is defined as ". . . a process of making certain the information needs of the people using the collection are met in a timely and economical manner, using information resources produced both inside and outside the organization" (Evans, 1987, p. 13). Collection development is not just equivalent to acquisition of documents but much more than that. Acquisition of documents consists of selection and procurement of documents. Document selection is central to the mission of the library. It is highly professional yet a 'pastoral work' (Pankake, 1984, p. 186). It is the document selection which over years has evolved into collection development and the selection decision continues to be the core of the activity. Acquisition work of a library involves three sets of people serendipitous methods like browsing stacks, talking to users, reviewing assorted catalogs, bibliographies, inter-library loan transactions, etc., it would not be wise to resort to 'retrospective collection development'. Without the feedback from systematic evaluation of the collections, review of users' needs and reacting to requests or complaints of patrons, retrospective selection becomes very difficult. If the original selection of library material is properly organised and the subsequent use and weeding properly monitored, there is no need for stock revision. Stock revision is less practised in special libraries than other types of libraries as they are likely to have less fluctuation in use, selections are invariably made by subject experts in special libraries and they are less likely to buy multiple copies (Spiller, 1980, p. 106). Each special library and its collection are unique.

There are many modes of acquisition of information resources, the most popular being the outright purchase. There are many methods within purchase mode of acquisition of information resources. They are approval plan or dealer library plan (mostly for books), bid, purchase of specific items against specific orders, blanket or standing orders, package deals, membership purchases, subscriptions, etc. The orders could be direct with publishers or through Indian or foreign agents including wholesalers wherever accessible or a combination of them. The modes of payment include advance payments, credit supply, payment against delivery, etc., depending on type of material being purchased and terms of suppliers.

Outright purchase is only part of the collection development strategy. 'Buy, beg, borrow or hire' at the least possible cost and time should be the objective of collection development in special libraries. Other modes of acquisition of information resources include free on request, unsought gratis/gift, rental, lease and exchange (which is more popular with gray literature like technical reports, pre-prints and reprints). One important aspect to be considered as integral part of collection development policy of a special library is policy of resource sharing with other libraries in the vicinity or region. Hence information resources can also be obtained on free loan through inter library cooperation. Lastly, rental or hire purchase is another mode of getting information resources, but it is not yet popular in Indian libraries.

The collection development policy should have clear guidelines

(Perkins, 1979) on the solicitation and acceptance of gifts as well as procedures for exchanges. Material acquired as gifts should meet the same standards as materials that are purchased. Hence gifts deserve and should receive the same care and processing as other materials. Normally, large part of gifts received are not useful as they are not in good physical condition and not consistent with the collection development plan. Libraries may have to have donor relations program which is periodically subjected to critical review. Apart from acknowledging gifts and helping donor to have tax benefits, if any, libraries have to make it clear to the donors that gifts will be used to the best advantage of libraries including exchanging, selling or discarding unwanted materials. Gifts may have to be politely rejected if necessary and by suggesting an alternative. Gifts and exchanges are useful ways of acquiring gray literature, disposing duplicates and discards. Unfortunately, Indian libraries practice exchanges of reading material to the least. There are no national exchange centres in the country. It is also true that often ". . . it is less expensive to buy books and serials than to obtain them on exchange" (Magrill and Hickey, 1984, p. 188).

No collection development policy or strategy is complete unless elements of coordinated or cooperative collection development and resource sharing are incorporated in it. "Cooperation, coordination, or sharing in the development and management of collection by two or more libraries entering into an agreement for this purpose" (Mosher and Pankake, 1983, p. 420) is called cooperative or coordinated collection development. Such cooperation or coordination should go hand in hand with resource sharing and networking. For effective and efficient resource sharing not only the factor militating against the philosophy of resource sharing should be respected but one also has to overcome the psychological and physical barriers. The concepts such as 'library without walls', 'library as a window of access then a fortress', need to provide access to information than ownership, learning to pay for services or use of information, collective ownership, buying information in new ways like digitised for a fax or tele fascimile are yet to be operationalised in this country. The tragedy of libraries in India is that coordinated or cooperative collection development and resource sharing are more talked than practiced. Neither libraries have overcome barriers to cooperation and resource sharing nor respected the factors which militate against resource sharing philosophy. Most of the libraries ask users, probably a selected representative sample population about their information requirements and needs. Such surveys are quite common in libraries. Opinion survey method basically puts the forecasting burden on users and the librarian merely persuades users to tell him what they feel as their requirement. It is not only necessary to discount unrealistic and exaggerated needs but also to identify unexpressed needs and try to supplement the data by adopting other more objective methods.

This method has several drawbacks. Firstly users may not be able to foresee, identify and express their needs in reasonably accurate terms. Secondly, they are likely to have strong likes, dislikes, fancies, idiosyncrasies and biases about what their library should possess. Thirdly, as this method heavily depends on sampling, questionnaire and/or interviewing techniques, it has all limitations of methodology. Fourthly, it is fairly expensive and time consuming. Lastly, this is a passive method in the sense that it lacks the vigour of marketing and fails to induce a desirable need in users and users often confine themselves to existing services.

2.1.2 *Survey of Collective Opinion of People Who Know Users*

This paternalistic approach presumes that librarians, information scientists, leaders, managers, planners, etc. know fairly accurately the needs of users. Since they are involved directly or indirectly in setting, identifying and promoting the objectives of the user community at large, they could be better predictors than actual users. A good example is information needs of R&D organisations. Unlike traditional industries, libraries do not normally overtly use this method.

Like user surveys, this method of collective opinion of people may also carry strong biases. Hence forecasted demands have to be further examined in the light of laid down objectives of the user groups, proposed changes, anticipated deviations and other factors of the environment.

This method is simple. The forecasts are based on first hand knowledge of people directly connected with the objectives of user group. It may prove quite useful or it may be the only method in case of new organisations. On the other hand it is fairly subjective as personal whims and fancies of a handful of people may be projected. Its utility is restricted to short term forecasting as people at this level may not remain for long time. Above all information needs cannot be thrusted upon actual users by any manager or leader.

2.1.3 *Study of Past Behaviour of Users*

A study of past behaviour of users could be directed towards actual users or users in similar environment elsewhere. In either case, specific case studies of user requirements emphasising need for information in various stages of work or project would be highly pertinent. This method heavily depends on data from indirect methods. Such studies help projecting trends in terms of both qualitative and quantitative demands. But they are often questioned about their capability to predict future behaviour and requirements of users, though there are a lot of for and against arguments that, as far as use of books are concerned, the past use determines the future use of books.

2.1.4 *Application of Statistical Techniques*

A wide spectrum of statistical techniques can be applied somewhat mechanically for forecasting demand for information in quantitative terms. A selected few are mentioned below. These techniques though applicable extensively to data from indirect methods, there is no bar in adopting them to data from direct methods such as questionnaire method.

The cheapest and easiest being 'Assume Constancy' which suffers from the drawbacks of rigid assumption of direct relation of the variables and ignoring the turning points. Another technique is 'Exponential Smoothening' which requires past quantitative data. This could form part of 'Time Series Analysis and Trend Projections'. Past data collected from a set of users who are actually seeking information arranged chronologically gives 'time series'. It is simple and inexpensive method based on the assumption that past rate of change of the variable under study will continue in the future. The assumption is alright till a turning point occurs. In case fluctuations and when turning points are faced, the factors responsible for characterising time series, i.e., trend, seasonal variations, cyclical fluctuation and irregular or random forces are to be analysed. The problem in forecasting is to separate and measure each of these four factors though such a decomposition of time series

As far as special libraries are concerned, the user community is a well defined small group. Yet the market analysis or needs assessment or community analysis requires an assessment of history, geography, transportation, legal, political, demographic, economic, communication, social, educational, cultural, recreational and other systems of the community as well as social indicators like age, sex, education, income, health, employment, marital status, etc.

It is possible to develop demand forecasting techniques for libraries on par with that of industry as described above. Many of these techniques are not new to librarianship, but differ only in nomenclature. The above mentioned methods are neither exhaustive nor mutually exclusive. In practice, one has to make wise decision in choosing a suitable method. A combination of two or more methods is often desirable when they can supplement and check each other. Whatever the technique, in all cases, one should bear in mind that the approach should be a unified approach of expertise and technique.

2.3 Assessing and Understanding Information Requirements of Users

User-research is the market-research in library and information science. Hence, the market-characteristics or customer-characteristics can be conveniently called user-characteristics. Marketing library services is something new to libraries. At the most, promoting of library services has taken place in the profession so far. Libraries which function with the motto of 'free service to all' can hardly claim selling or marketing its services. It is meaningless to market a free service or product. Being paternalistic systems, libraries try to create awareness among users and persuade them to use information, documents and other library services which they think are needed by their users. Hence, the term 'market' mean the predetermined domain of customers of libraries as per the laid down objectives and not in the broad sense in which a typical businessman uses it. No doubt that market-research (user-research) and customer (user) behaviour studies are essential for libraries (Sridhar, 1988).

The information-requirements refer to a lookout for a sort of relevance of information to a given user and to his areas of concern and interest, likes and dislikes. Relevance is not a simple property inherent in information, but varies with content, format, context, the variety of uses of information as well as user himself (Cott, 1970). "The selection and reception of the information will depend upon the individual's conception of his own needs; one man's information is another man's noise. . . ." (McGarry, 1975, p. 58).

There have been numerous studies as well as reviews about user-needs and requirements, but with little accumulation of body of knowledge. Meaning, scope, levels and types of information-needs have varied very widely. Problems of defining terms and concepts, lack of theoretical frameworks and other problems and issues of an empirical study of information needs and requirements persist (Brittain, 1971, p. 2). The successive reviewers like Menzel, Martyn and Crawford have pointed out (in ARIST, 1966, 1974 and 1978) the extremely complex, varied and difficult-to-measure nature of information-need. Menzel has even preferred to call 'information needs and uses' as a study of the behaviour and experiences of scientists and technologists. Hatt (1976, p. 42-43) called them 'user behaviour studies' and Wilson (1981) advocated that the term 'information-needs' should be replaced by 'information-seeking towards the satisfaction of needs.'

While discussing the issue of information-needs, a natural assumption is to consider the needs as perceived by the users. But some are of the view that there is a need to create information-needs among users if they do not exist (Harris, 1985, p. 2) and that information-seekers may be ignorant of the information that would be useful to them (Oldman, 1976, p. 23).

Dervin (1976) has analysed the taxonomy of everyday information-needs of average citizen and proposed a study of six linkages among the following four elements: (1) The individual citizen, (2) Information-needs, (3) Information sources, (4) Solutions to information-needs. Each one of the linkage represents interaction between two elements. Havelock (1976, p. 211) provided a linkage model/process describing the internal problem-solving cycle within a user who is related to an external resource.

As noted earlier, Information-needs are affected by many factors. Range and knowledge of information-sources/facilities available, varieties of uses to which information will be put, the background, motivation, professional orientation, discipline, type and area of work and other individual-characteristics of the user, the social, political and economic system as well as the consequences of information-use (Cronin, 1981, p. 39; Lin and Garvey, 1972, p. 8-10). Due to this slightly science-oriented work has resulted in increased need for information, particularly, theoretical background and basic S & T information.

2.4.2 *Future Information Requirements*

A free discussion with selected space technologists about their future information requirements revealed that a large majority (over 60%) do not foresee any significant change in their information requirements in the near future. Even if there is a little change they do not find it difficult to adapt to the circumstances over time. Out of the rest who thought of some changes in their information requirements in future, some expressed their fear at the problem of availability of increased quantity of information than what one could digest (i.e., the problem of 'information overload'). This is not merely because of increased production of information, but because of enlargement of boundaries of interest and activities of the organisation. Others thought of the impact of electronics boom and some others explained how the organisation has to intensify its activities, increase its capabilities, reliability, quality and hence risks. The outcome of the discussion is that they are recognising the need for some condensed information services, new media of information and fast serving information agents. A sort of digesting agents as intermediary professionals are likely to come up in the core teams of projects both to cut short delays and face the problem of information-overload.

2.5 Collection Development based on Needs of Information Staff and Information Functions and Services

Apart from systematic forecasting of demand and broad understanding of needs and requirements of users, it is also necessary to identify needs of information staff and others concerned with information functions and services in a special library for development of appropriate collection. Many information resources like reference books and secondary journals are mainly used by information staff as intermediaries and hence collection development has to take care of needs of information men i.e. library staff and requirements of information services and functions like abstracting, indexing, translating, technical inquiry, information searching and reference services. This also necessitates an active participation of information staff in collection building process.

The role of users, library staff and library management/ committee in development of collection varies from library to library. The responsibilities of library staff and library management in collection development is obvious and assumed. But active participation of users in collection development is highly desired. In a sense user participation in collection development indirectly reveals the 'market penetration' of the library. The relative merits and implications of participation of users, staff and management in collection development are yet to be clearly established.

NOTES

1. Based on the replies from national members, WFEO (1979, p. 21) identified eight types of data most needed by engineers i.e., (i) property, (ii) design, (iii) product, (iv) standards, regulations and laws, (v) production and manufacturing procedures, (vi) companies and their marketing products, (vii) market information and (viii) socio-economic and ecology information.
2. An index was developed for each person in the population based on various quantifiable professional activities and achievements like lectures delivered, conferences attended, reports prepared, papers published, patents obtained, awards received, membership in professional bodies, official tours, journals subscribed, committees represented, in-service trainings received, part-time studies undertaken, etc., in a specified period adjusted to length of experience.

(b) Suggestions for periodicals are mostly one time suggestions;

(c) Browsing report announcement bulletins such as STAR, GRA&I, BRTT, etc., is generally done by limited number of users;

(d) Reports themselves being highly specialised in nature, a typical report is expected to be required by a very small set of users.

Again from Table 3.1 one can see that about 40 to 51 per cent of users suggested only one item per year. Similarly, 16 to 23 per cent suggested two and 10 to 11 per cent suggested three items. Interestingly, about 25 per cent (i.e., 41 users) have suggested 64 per cent (i.e. 317) books, reports and periodicals and only 198 users directly participated in the collection building process. Library had about 800 technical staff of the organisation as registered members and more than 1,200 total users during 1982. Thus, the direct and active participation in collection building was made only by less than 25 per cent of users.

TABLE 3.1: Frequency Distribution of Number of Suggestions Over Number of Users

No. of Suggestions	Books		Reports		Periodicals	
	No. of Users	Total Sugges-tions	No. of Users	Total Sugges-tions	No. of Users	Total Sugges-tions
1	80 (49%)	80	18 (40%)	18	24 (51%)	24
2	27 (16%)	54	9 (20%)	18	11 (23%)	22
3	16 (10%)	48	5 (11%)	15	5 (11%)	15
4	8	32	1	4	2	8
5	8	40	3	15	2	10
6	5	30	2	12	0	0
7	6	42	3	21	2	14
8	1	8	0	0	0	0
9	2	18	1	9	1	9
10	3	30	2	20	0	0
11	0	0	0	0	0	0
12	2	24	0	0	0	0
13	1	13	0	0	0	0
14	1	14	1	14	0	0
15	1	15	0	0	0	0
16	1	16	0	0	0	0
17	1	17	0	0	0	0
18	1	18	0	0	0	0
Total	164	499	45	146	47	102

3.3 Extent of User-Participation in Collection Development

While the overall user-participation in collection development is less than 25 per cent, the ratio of user suggested items to total items ordered by the library during the year is presented in Table 3.2. As could be seen from the table, on this count also, the user-participation in collection development is quite low. Hardly, 18 to 35 per cent of the items ordered (other than standing orders, abstracting, indexing, free and ephemeral periodicals) by the Library are based on direct suggestions from users. Orders for the rest of the items were as a result of document selection work of library staff and Library Committee.

TABLE 3.2: Comparison of User-Suggestions with Total Items Ordered

Document type	Total No. of items ordered	Items suggested by users		Duplicates		Users Participated		Average suggestions per user
		No.	%	No.	%	No.	%	
Books	1046*	366	31.99	133	36.34	164	20.50	3.04
Reports	513*	145	28.27	1	0.65	45	5.63	3.24
Periodicals	552@	102	18.48	0	0.00	47	5.88	2.17

Key: * Excludes standing orders.
@ Excludes abstracting, indexing, free and ephemeral periodicals.

Though duplicate or repeated suggestions for reports and periodicals are almost nil, the suggestions for books had duplication to the extent of 36 per cent. This is mainly due to display of books received on approval basis and book exhibitions attracting simultaneously more than one user for many books of common interest and for other reasons such as specific nature of reports, etc., explained earlier.

It may also be seen from Table 3.2 that, the percentage of users who participated in collection building is little over 5 for reports and periodicals and 20.5 for books. Lastly, average number of suggestions per user per year is around 2 to 3 and this itself is an indication of low user-participation in collection development.

3.4 Reasons for Low Participation of Users

Although probing into reasons for low participation of users in acquisition methods.

Contrary to the above situation, if a library is not located in one of the major cities or capital of the state, it lacks quick and easy access to the stock of the vendors to make best choice of off-the-shelf-documents. Further, it may not be economical to have more than 3 or 4 vendors for approval or dealer library plan. As such vendor selection poses serious problem to many libraries (see 4.3.2).

4.2.4 *Inadequate Product Specification*

Fourthly, as mentioned earlier, the details of the documents (other than books received on approval) is so inadequate that confident selection cannot be made even by the subject expert. Unless first hand knowledge of the contents of the document with its bibliographic characteristics are made available, selector may not be able to do justice for selection or deselection of the document. The announcements of vendors usually lack year of publication, edition, publisher and other details of documents. Most of the announcements of Indian vendors are for off-the-shelf costly books. Inadequate information about documents constraints pre order searching to establish existence of an item as well as to establish the need for an item.

4.2.5 *Lack of Information about Cheaper Editions*

Another serious problem coming in the way of economical acquisition of documents is the lack of correct and timely information about availability of the latest editions, low priced/Indian/paperback editions. This problem together with the differentiated pricing policies and deliberate manipulation of some vendors in avoiding supply of cheaper editions leads to inefficient purchases.

4.2.6 *Lack of Confirmed Prices*

Yet another peculiar situation under which document selection has to be made is non-availability of confirmed price of a document at the time of selection. Unfortunately, publishers and suppliers keep the right to revise the price till the date of billing/supply. This also adds to problems of fiscal management (4.3.10) paralysing the monitoring of budget and expenditure.

4.2.7 *Need for Avoiding Duplication*

A very crucial problem of document acquisition is avoiding duplication in the collection. This assumes additional significance in special libraries where collection has to be compact. The duplication may appear in the form of duplicate copies of documents, different editions (with or without revision) of the same document and it may be substantial content duplication among different documents. As far as duplicate copies are concerned one can have a thorough checking with existing stock, on order files and 'just received but not processed' files and reach almost 99.5 per cent success depending on accuracy and completeness of available information. Deciding the key element and procedure for rendering key element (say author) for pre-order searching become highly significant for elimination of duplicates. The acquisitions librarian has to be doubly careful about different editions of the same documents. Having known the traditional approach of the libraries to treat different editions of a book as fresh/different book many publishers do print new editions either with cosmetic changes or without any changes. The duplication arising out of contents has to be checked only with the help of subject experts and users. However, the duplication due to reappearance in different forms like special issue of a journal and a book, journal article and conference paper, thesis, report and book, at times is difficult to check.

For all these reasons it would not be wrong if one says that a sort of blind man's choice takes place in document selection without really knowing how much is being paid for how much of utility of the product.

4.3 Document Procurement Problems

Having seen some of the problems faced at the time of selection of documents, the problems related to the document procurement transactions are discussed below. The foremost task and problem in procurement activity of a special library is to determine the vendors of all types of materials, their terms, credibility, efficiency and service. One has to be aware of bogus companies and individuals in the trade and continuously evaluate vendors based on sample orders and other criteria. A special library has to sequence its orders in such a way that a steady stream of documents arrive at regular intervals in the library.

telephone or telex charges levied by foreign suppliers are too heavy and disproportional to the cost of the material being supplied. Some times airfreight and other expenses like foreign postage, custom clearance charges, etc., are also arbitrarily levied by local suppliers too. Another peculiar tactics of obscure publishers and suppliers within the country is to send books by VPP or by freight-to-pay basis without proper order from libraries.

Just like suppliers are born overnight both within the country and abroad, there are companies abroad who go for liquidation in short time and claims of libraries are passed on to their chartered accountants. Of course within the country it is difficult even to locate the liquidated supplier or his chartered accountant. Only a prolonged endless court proceedings will be left with for a library to recover dues, if any.

4.4 Collection Development in Languages other than English

It is well known that nearly half of science and technology information is in languages other than English. Science and technology literature in Indian languages may be negligible, but it needs to be given sufficient support by acquiring, organising and disseminating in special libraries. Book selection tools and sources of supply for books in Indian languages are highly inadequate.

Development of collection in languages other than English in general and Indian languages in particular depends largely on knowledge of such languages among users and availability of in-house and/or external translation facilities and the willingness and capabilities of special libraries in providing such translation services. There is no meaning in acquiring large collection in foreign languages which are not known to its users and where there are no translation facilities. On the other hand, subscribing to current awareness services and secondary journals which provide information about existence of English translations of foreign language documents aids the in-house translation unit to check availability of English translation before undertaking translation or ordering translation with external agency as well as users to browse foreign language literature in English. This is only one of the instances which describes close relation between various information functions and services and collection development in special libraries.

4.5 Problems of Publishers and Vendors

All alternate solutions to problems are not discussed here. Nor the problems discussed are exhaustive. There are many significant, probably contradictory versions of problems of suppliers too. Though they are outside the purview of this book, a few major problems of suppliers and vendors to be kept in mind by librarians are mentioned here briefly. First of all settling approval memos in about 30–45 days is fervently sought by vendors. Of course, each library can afford to have a selected small number of vendors instructed to send highly selective set of books on approval basis to meet precise requirements of the library and also to avoid frittering away of energy in sorting, displaying, selecting/rejecting same set of books from many vendors.

As mentioned earlier, most important problem of suppliers and the responsibility of acquisitions librarian is to arrange payment of credit supply bills in about 30–45 days. Prompt payments only ensure easy cash flow to vendors. Other problems which are mounting on suppliers and vendors are hike in foreign postage, reduction in trade discount by publishers, unmindful rejection of journal claims by publishers, increase in bank charges, postal pilferages/transit losses, operational costs, incidental expenses, cost of stationary and other overheads. They also face problems where requirements are not precisely described and orders of libraries do not carry a mix of easy as well as difficult items.

In recent years, publishers are caught in a vicious circle of increase in costs of material and labour leading to increase in prices of reading material on the one side and steady cut in sales due to increased prices, inflation, budgetary constraints and resource sharing arrangements of institutional buyers on the other. Paper and administrative works at publishers and vendors end add to the cost of the reading materials.

Another peculiar problem of vendors is the practice of dual system of trade i.e., producer to wholesaler to retailer to buyer concept is not strictly followed in the trade. Buyer can directly interact with publisher or wholesaler in addition to retailer.

5

BOOK PROCUREMENT DELAYS:
A Case Study

In a case study of user-participation in collection development in Chapter 3, it was revealed that 35 per cent of total acquisition of books were against specific suggestions of users and only about 21 per cent of total users have ever suggested books to ISAC Library. It was also observed that one of the reasons for such a low participation of users in collection development is book procurement delays. Quick and timely procurement of suggested/on-demand books act as achievement motivator for further suggestions from users. On the other hand, procurement delays could be dangerous disincentives to the meager 21 per cent of users participating in collection development activity.

Delays in providing on-demand books to users have two major components. Firstly, order processing, classifying, cataloguing and other processing delays at library, which mainly depend on the work environment of the library including quantum of work, available trained manpower and efficiency of the staff. Yet at this stage, by allowing 'line clear treatment' to such books delays can be minimised. The second type of delays are at the book trade/suppliers end and this delay is substantially beyond the control of a library.

A case study is presented here to show the extent of delays on the part of book suppliers for on-demand books. Incidentally the case study also helps by providing some guidelines for future book procurement policy of the Library.

Before analysing the data one should take note of the background of the data in terms of procurement policies of the library and limitations of the data. Supply position of books ordered by ISAC Library during 1983 were analysed as of mid September 1984. Orders for theses and reports, standing orders, orders based on approval books and ready stock announcements were excluded from the study for obvious reasons. Most of the orders were placed on more than a dozen carefully selected, fairly known vendors, both Indian and foreign, including exclusive/specialised dealers and direct suppliers. Few orders placed on miscellaneous suppliers are clubbed with direct suppliers in the analysis. Most of the orders made directly on publishers required advance payments unlike credit supply terms of other vendors.

Further, some of the outstation suppliers within the country supply through VPP or Railway parcel or road parcel involving additional marginal delay. Though originally data was tabulated month-wise it was not found much useful as it was not the purpose to analyse the data for 'how soon' books are supplied. On the other hand, taking for granted that there will be some delay, 'how many' books are supplied within a period of 8 to 20 months is examined in the analysis. Hence data is grouped for four quarters of 1983 in Table 5.1.

In addition, the following limitations of the table may be noted. Firstly, all the books for which there are specialised/exclusive representatives were ordered on such Indian suppliers, i.e., IS1, IS2 and IS3 in Table 5.1. Out of the remaining, books of popular publishers such as Academic, Pergamon and McGraw-Hill were ordered in batches almost together on Indian suppliers (i. e., IS4 to IS10) with the hope of getting many such books quickly from ready stock. Thirdly, as far as possible, each Indian supplier was provided with orders representing books of all popular publishers. Yet supply position is not analysed here by publisher of the book. Fourthly, most of the books of professional bodies (so called short discount titles) were directly ordered with publishers including Indian publishers i. e., IS11 and DS3. Fifthly, rest of the books including books of less known/obscure publishers and books which are not likely to be available in local market were ordered with two foreign suppliers (FS1 and FS2 in the table), one in U.K. and the other in U.S.A., based on the nationality and pricing policy of the publishers. Sixthly, all orders except orders made during first quarter were for recently published books. Substantial number of books ordered during first quarter were published during 1970s. Lastly, data is found slightly inadequate in case of suppliers IS3 and IS5. So is the case with third and fourth quarter orders on Indian retailers.

TABLE 5.1 Supply Status of On-Demand Books Ordered during 1983

Month of Order		Indian Suppliers: Exclusive/Specialised IS1	IS2	IS3	S. Total No.	%	Indian Suppliers: Retailers IS4	IS5	IS6	IS7	IS8	IS9	IS10	Direct & Misc. IS11	S. Total No.	%	Foreign Suppliers: Retailers FS1	FS2	Direct & Misc. FS3	S. Total No.	%	Grand Total No.	%
Jan-Mar	O	0	13	0	13		18	0	21	26	22	24	32	6	149		18	0	39	57		219	
	S	0	13	0	13	100	3	0	8	6	6	3	6	3	35	13	15	0	22	37	65	85	39
Apr-Jun	O	9	14	1	24		3	7	1	5	3	0	10	15	44		31	21	32	84		152	
	S	9	14	1	24	100	2	1	1	1	3	0	0	4	12	27	26	14	12	52	68	88	59
Jul-Sep	O	6	2	0	8		0	0	0	4	0	0	4	30	38		60	27	60	147		193	
	S	5	2	0	7	88	0	0	0	0	0	0	0	15	15	39	45	22	34	10	69	23	64
Oct-Dec	O	29	6	8	43		0	0	0	0	0	0	3	2	5		62	51	93	206		154	
	S	21	5	2	28	65	0	0	0	0	0	0	2	1	3	60	40	20	39	99	40	90	61
Total	O	44	35	9	88		21	7	22	35	25	24	49	53	226		171	99	224	494		618	
	S	35	34	3	72	82	5	1	9	7	9	3	8	23	65	28	126	56	107	299	59	426	62
	%	80	97	33	82		24	14	41	20	36	13	16	43	28		74	57	48	59		62	

Key: O = Ordered quantity; S = Supplied Quantity; S. Total = Sub Total.

It may be seen from Table 5.1 that out of 818 on-demand books ordered during 1983, only 426 (i.e., 52%) were supplied by September 1984. This is against the usual tall claim of the industry that any book published anywhere in the world can be supplied in about six months time. In other words, 48 per cent of demands of users are not met even after 8/20 months of placing orders. By and large, exclusive/specialised agents have fared fairly better with an overall 82 per cent efficiency. The performance of foreign vendors with an average of 59 per cent efficiency is much better than 28 per cent efficiency of Indian vendors. It may be noted here that though foreign vendors have unilaterally cancelled some titles after lapse of six months/one year, the same are not excluded from the data. Among Indian vendors, highest percentage (i.e., 42%) of books have been bought by direct orders including orders on miscellaneous suppliers. The next highest performance among Indian vendors are by IS6 (41%) (though data is inadequate to generalise) and IS1 (36%).

Among foreign vendors FS1 has been quite better with 74 per cent efficiency than FS2 which supplied 59 per cent of books. However, direct and miscellaneous suppliers (FS3) could supply only 48 per cent understandably due to infrequent contacts of the library and lengthy advance payment procedure involved. Looking at the table for row totals one can see the supply position of orders made during different quarters of 1983. For convenience Table 5.2 presents, by extracting from Table 5.1, percentages of on-demand books supplied by Indian and foreign suppliers for orders of four quarters of 1983. An interesting observation is that the percentage of books supplied is not at all directly proportional to time as far as Indian retail vendors are concerned. However, supply of exclusive/specialised Indian dealers and foreign suppliers show a trend that more books are supplied against older orders. In fact, a reverse trend of more supplies against recent orders than old orders is seen in case of Indian retail vendors. This goes to confirm the general observation that many Indian book vendors make random supply in an accidental way, depending on match of pending orders with stock based on memory of operating staff. There were instances where books pending for supply for long time came as books on approval either from the same vendor or others in the city. As such old orders may not materialise fully and reach 90 to 95 per cent supply even after 2-3 years. Even the feedback about delay or non-availability or cancellation comes rarely from Indian vendors.

Vendors should respond with a meaningful report when they cannot fulfill an order within a reasonable period and not with standing and vague replies like 'temporarily out of stock'. With the mushrooming of retail book vendors and certain problems of the trade no sign of improvement in supply position of on-demand books is seen in the near future. They try to concentrate on fairly costly books, standing orders on serials, books of popular publishers and prefer dealer library (approval) plan to promote what is available (or what is left?) in their stock than meeting on-demand requirements of users. Very few of them have systematic methods of informing libraries about status of supply and non-supply to enable libraries to take alternate action. In this respect, foreign vendors are quite prompt. With their computerised system, they inform libraries about status of supply as well as cancellation after lapse of stipulated period. Few years ago, a similar experiment was done by ISAC Library with Indian wholesale dealers and the result was not much different from that of Indian retail vendors. Under the circumstances, special libraries may have to explore newer methods of acquiring on-demand books like obtaining by bulk airfreight and/or selective airmail from foreign vendors once convinced about non-availability in local market.

TABLE 5.2: Summary of supply status of On-Demand Books (as of September 1984)

Month of Order	Suppliers			Total
	Indian		Foreign	
	Exclusive/ Specialised	Retailers		
Jan-Mar 1983	100	23	65	59
Apr-Jun 1983	100	27	62	58
Jul-Sep 1983	88	39	69	64
Oct-Dec 1983	65	60	48	51
Total	[illegible]	[illegible]	59	52

Note: All figures are in percentages.

Knowing where a library stands in terms of procurement of on-demand books and using the results to frame future procurement policies are necessary. Since users are not much concerned with the problems faced by libraries due to delays at book trade/suppliers end, all the delays have to be apparently absorbed as delays at library and the acquisitions librarian has to smilingly say user is always right. The problem of procurement delays persists to a great extent.

6

TECHNICAL REPORTS COLLECTION

It has been established that the scientific communication, particularly communication in physical sciences, first flows through the informal channel and then perhaps after development and modification, through the formal channel (Garvey, 1970, p. 1170). The informal communication being interactive, user directed, speedy, economical and secured, has claimed heavy reliance on it as a major source of information. But, exclusive dependence on it may lead to inadequate coverage, inaccurate results, duplication of efforts, bibliographic chaos and retardation of growth of science and technology. Thus evolved a semi-formal literature incorporating many advantages of both formal and informal communication. "A substantial and specialised segment of the semi-formal literature consists of technical reports" (National Academy of Sciences and National Academy of Engineering, 1969, p. 115). In other words, certain informal functions of scientific and technical communication are formalised by reports to enhance the effectiveness of communication. Primary journals and technical reports are two important media for primary communication in science and technology. In spite of downgrading and non-recognition by established periodicals, technical reports have gained equal or even more importance than periodicals in recent years. There was a time when publishers and editors of scientific periodicals refused to accept articles based on technical reports and did not even allow authors to cite reports. As a result the publication of original results or ideas in technical reports was considered a professional hazard. Interestingly, "the scientist, as a producer of information is . . . interested in seeing his work published in a prestigious journal, [but] the scientist, as a user of information, is much less concerned with the way in which it is presented" (Brearley, 1973, p. 117). However, the era of exclusive S&T communication through periodicals has almost ceased for various reasons.

It is widely accepted that a precise definition of technical report cannot be given, though report can be recognised by sight. Most of the definitions of report are descriptive. Further the boundary of reports literature is vague and it depends much on individual interpretations. There is substantial overlapping of functions of different forms of literature with technical reports.

Use of reports for internal communication and exchange of reports among scientists existed as early as in 16th century. More reports were brought out during mid-19th century as a result of large scale industrial application of science and technology. However, reports in its present and distinct form of communication is a 20th century phenomenon. Professional papers of the USGS (1902), technological papers of the NBS (1910), and reports and memoranda of Advisory Committee for Aeronautics (1909, now called ARC) and NACA (1914) are some of the earliest reports. The growth of reports was much accelerated during World War II when Government investment in science based industries increased vastly giving impetus to more research, especially defence and industry oriented research. This thrust on research coupled with the need for rapid communication immensely felt by industries, defence and other Government agencies, has brought numerous reports (Kent and Lancour 1980, p. 147; Hartas, 1967 p. 80-81).

"About 80-85 per cent of the world's report literature is of US origin and probably over 90 per cent of reports of US and foreign origin go through the input end of five US agencies, namely, DDC, NASA, DOE, NTIS and ERIC, even if they do not reach the output point" (Chillag, 1970, p. 201-202; Chillag, 1973, p. 39-40). "By 1950 results of (US) Government sponsored research were being published in reports at the rate of 75,000 to 1,00,000 a year" (Godfrey and Redman, 1973 p. 2). There is no accurate estimate of number of reports produced at present. The estimates vary from 1,00,000 to 5,00,000 per year (Kent and Lancour [1980] may be seen for different estimates).

Volumes have been written about technical reports and it is obvious even from a partial survey of literature that reports have created more controversies and problems than any other form of literature. What is more important is almost anything said about reports can be argued to be true. One may say reports are bulky or thin, shabby or good, important or unimportant, one could still be right. In other words, reports are unusual and heterogeneous in many respects. They are quasi published, semi-formal and semi-restricted and they fall in between books and periodical articles in size, share many characteristics of pre-prints, reappear many a times as periodical articles, conference papers and monographs.

The rapidly growing report literature is the outcome of certain definite needs of information transfer process. Reports come very handy for communication of internally generated information within an organisation or from contractor to funding agency. Enormous data and information generated in the normal course of work of R&D organisations are presented in the form of reports. Success of a special library can be partly measured by its capacity to provide internally generated information. Apart from avoiding duplication of work, internal reports, if handled properly, help amicable settling of agreements with outside organisations for exchange of reports.

The formal primary communication channels of information are very much choked and cannot effectively accommodate very large quantity of information, often un-edited and unabridged, arising out of high rate of technological advancement and high pressure of large scale R&D. If only adequate formal means of communication existed for scientific and technical information, reports would not have gained the importance we see today. As mentioned in the beginning, many advantages of informal communication such as rapid and effective transfer of information also contributed to the popularity of reports.

Technical reports are bestowed with many advantages. Owing to their easy, quick and flexible method of production they have enabled issuing agencies to bring out short run editions. Even bulky reports can be produced quickly and cheapl, in small quantities by simple mimeographing or offset printing. The microfiche has made this much more simpler. The absence of refereeing, quality control checks, unrestricted form, format and volume have further added greater speed to publication of reports. Reports stand out for their timeliness, speed and for providing most current and up to date information. They are normally faster than other primary media. It is said "that as vehicles for dissemination of technical information, technical reports are much faster than journal articles" (Kent and Lancour, 1980, p. 146). Sargent stressing the expensive nature of medical research, expresses the importance of technical reports in the following way: "If the technical report, by its very nature, can be issued several months to several years in advance of its appearance in a journal, then it seems to me that we are not doing a thorough job of

agencies that it become very costly to avail services of such agencies. Even librarians may have to spare substantial time and efforts to study and understand wantonly made complexities, content duplication and discriminated pricing policies of these agencies. This dependence on agencies of information rich countries is steadily increasing. India too is potentially rich, but lacks national agency to organise and explore this resource. At present many of Indian R&D reports can be more easily located and purchased from agencies of information rich countries than within the country. The situation is well exploited and encashed by foreign agencies and their Indian agents.

Proliferation of report numbers, microforms, organisation of internal reports, barriers of security-classification, lack of quality control, bibliographic control, content duplication, noise, procurement and organisation of reports are practical problems of special libraries. Though initially editors of scientific periodicals have discouraged reports and documentalists have not given due status to reports, the report handling agencies have brought archival status to reports. "Notwithstanding the controversy over their status, technical reports are becoming increasingly important as vehicles for the dissemination of technical information" (Kent and Lancour, 1980, p. 156).

Reports are the major let-outs of R&D engineers and technologists who depend heavily on intra-corporate sources of information with less autonomy in choice of projects as against academicians and scientists who not only have wider choice of topics but also communications, both inside and outside the undertaking, and should be given preferential treatment in special libraries (Hartas, 1967, p. 86). Looking at the trend that increasing coverage of reports by secondary periodicals and use of reports in social sciences, it is strongly urged that "the technical reports should now be accorded full recognition as an established form of technical literature and should be granted the rights therefrom by those handling that literature" (Godfrey and Redman, 1973, p. 1).

6.1 A Case Study of Collection Development of Technical Reports

As a first step in building reports collection at ISAC library, more than 200 organisations throughout the world dealing with space science, space technology, satellite technology and allied areas were contacted for supply of reports on exchange or gratis. While about 35 organisations responded positively, some declined the request on security grounds, and others said that their documents may not be useful to ISAC Library users. A few important organisations, whose reports are of high significance to ISAC Library users, could not be contacted as they are either defence organisations or already had arrangements for exchange of reports with parent organisation, namely, ISRO. However, reports received by ISRO Head Quarters at Bangalore are also made available to ISAC library. Some are transferred, some are issued on loan and some given in the form of xerox copies. Inter-library loan arrangements with libraries of other ISRO Centres and a few local libraries also exist. Few 'core' organisations producing reports of interest to ISAC library users are NASA, ESA, DFVLR, CNES, ONERA, COSPAR, AGARD, NASDA, etc. Parallel action was also taken to develop collection of unclassified and unrestricted internal reports. For various reasons, including problems of security and lack of screening mechanism, the collection of internal reports in the library is not exhaustive. Scientists and engineers of the Centre have donated many useful reports acquired by them through personal contacts.

A long term plan was made to purchase reports with the objective of not missing any significant report of current or future interest to the organisation. An indirect estimate based on intake of NTIS revealed that about 12,000 reports of interest to ISAC Library users are produced every year and their number roughly grows at the rate of 10 per cent per year. This estimate is subject to the interpretation of the scope of subject categories and sub-categories of NTIS and the actual process of matching incoming reports against profile. To acquire 12,000 reports at the prevailing (in 1979) average price, about Rs.17 lakhs per year was needed. In addition, the library had to acquire many old reports against demand. Such a huge budget for reports alone was not available and appeared disproportionately high. At this juncture, it was decided to go in for the subscription or standing order service of the NTIS like the SRIM service for supply of relevant full text reports in microfiche on a bi-weekly basis. This service started from June 1979 and brought more than 4,000 reports in 1979 for Rs. 40,000, about 14,000 reports in 1980 for Rs. 2,00,000 and 7,000 reports in 1981 for Rs. 1,10,000. In addition to this, an expenditure varying from Rs. 40,000 to Rs.85,000 per year was incurred during 1979 to 1981 on paper copy reports. The profile for

SRIM service was continuously evaluated and refined in the light of feedback from users and budget constraints over years. It is now tightly defined and the resultant reduction in in-take of reports is reduced twice by about 50 per cent in last 10 years. Today, ISAC Library has more than 70,000 microfiche reports and 10,000 paper copy reports in the collection. Of late, many paper copy reports are produced within the library from microfiche copies leading to considerable reduction in in-take of paper copy reports from commercial sources.

6.1.1 *Technical Reports in Microform*

The decision to buy microfiche reports as against paper copy reports needs a little more elaboration. No doubt, by opting for microfiche, up to 90 per cent on actual price of reports and more than 90 per cent of storing space were saved. The most interesting aspect is that these reports were supplied to the Library by air-freight without additional charges and they reached the Library much earlier than the secondary periodical (GRA&I) of NTIS which announces these reports. The magnitude of saving with microfiche reports can be realised if one examines the price schedule and the mandatory air freight charges of NTIS for paper copies. Problems of procurement of paper copy technical reports are enumerated later in this chapter.

However, it would be necessary to mention here about extra costs involved in terms of additional facility and other disadvantages in using microfiche reports. A major hindrance in developing and using microfiche collection is user reluctance. Undoubtedly reports collection would have been utilised much more intensively if the entire collection was in paper form. Added to this, storing and air conditioning facilities and supporting user equipment have to be provided. Eventhough standardisation, compatibility, quality control and other problems are not faced with the medium reduction (24X and 48X) microfiche of NMA Type 1 and Type 7 acquired so far, non-availability of good indigenous user equipment, storing, cleaning and writing aids is retarding the promotion of microforms. An imported user equipment facility developed consists of micrographics markers, cleaning equipment and consumables, care kit, hand held viewers (operating on both AC and DC), portable readers (with chargeable battery), table top readers and enlarger printers. Problems and prospects of microforms are presented in greater detail in the next chapter.

6.2 Procurement of Technical Reports

Importance of technical reports for mission and problem oriented research such as space science and satellite technology, energy, education, environment, etc. need not be overemphasised. Reports are normally not handled in the traditional way through the channels of book trade though there are book-sellers acting as agents for some clearing houses. There is enormous duplication among sources and selection tools of reports. At the same time there is no single source, single selection tool and single mode of procurement of reports which can efficiently and effectively meet the requirements of a library. An attempt is made here to highlight the problems faced by Indian libraries in acquiring reports with suitable illustrations drawn from the case study of ISAC Library.

6.2.1 *Procurement Methods*

Unclassified, declassified and unrestricted reports can be acquired in many ways. Normally free initial distribution of limited number of copies of such reports is done by publications department or library of the organisation which brings out report. Contractors decide the list for free distribution in case of contract reports. Some agencies continue to supply reports even after initial distribution. Others redirect all requests for free copies to authorised depositors or clearinghouses such as NTIS, USGPO, HMSO, etc., which are responsible for secondary distribution of reports.

Firstly, considerable number of reports come to library as unsought supply due to institutional or individual affiliation or contacts or membership with a committee or organisation. Secondly, users themselves donate reports which they often receive free. Thirdly, the library after deliberate scanning of announcement bulletins of reports such as STAR, GRA&I, BRTT, R&D Abstracts (now ceased), etc., and also based on suggestions received from users, contact issuing agencies for free supply of reports. Catching reports as gifts while they are in initial distribution stage is naturally the least expensive method.

ISAC Library as well as parent organisation have tried and settled few bilateral agreements with other similar organisations and agencies for exchange of reports. Success of such agreements normally depend on keeping exchange process alive. It also depends on how many reports can be offered by an organisation and how much relevant and useful they are to the receiving organisation. National and international depositories and clearing houses could not be involved in such a program by the Library. Lastly, one important caution in acquiring reports as gifts or on exchange basis is that library should resist temptation to receive and retain ephemeral and irrelevant reports.

Before proceeding to buy reports, one should carefully consider borrowing reports from other libraries and xeroxing wherever they are not copyrighted. This is a crucial step as many commercial suppliers also provide only xerox copies of reports at exorbitant rates involving precious foreign exchange. Wherever allowed, one should prefer to make a single copy for non-commercial use from copies available as a means of quick service. As mentioned earlier, occasionally microfiche copies of reports, in addition to sizable microfiche reports received as part of SRIM service of NTIS, are also bought at ISAC Library and paper copies made with the in-house facility. This is also very economical method next only to 'gift' and 'exchange' methods discussed above. At times reports are supplied only in microfiche form forcing a library to acquire them in microfiche form only. ISAC Library also has a standing order with NTIS for NASA formal series reports to be supplied as and when published and they are often received much earlier than other methods of procurement. A later Chapter discusses the problems of this standing order together with its evaluation. All other reports needed by users are purchased from various commercial sources. Operating deposit or charge account (e.g. USGPO) and coupon system (e.g. BLLD) apart from contacting parent organisations for free supply are quite appropriate for gray literature and society publications in general and technical reports in particular.

6.2.2 *Procurement Problems*

So far, different methods of procurement of reports are discussed without highlighting the problems. Summarising the general problems of so called gray literature which includes reports Wood (1982 p. 460) says ". . . its distribution is haphazard, it is produced in limited quantities and it is not subject to rigorous quality control either at the editing or production stage. As such, it is difficult to discover, difficult to acquire, often difficult to store, frequently difficult to read and difficult to copy". Major problems of Indian libraries in procuring technical reports will be discussed under the heads bibliographic control and access, avoiding duplication, efficiency and effectiveness of suppliers, problems of economy, problems relating to physical conditions, report series codes, security classification, etc. It is also worth noting that report literature accounts for a significant portion of gray literature and US generates more report literature than any other country (Vickers, 1982, p. 502). Hence NTIS with about 50 per cent of input from quasi-government or government sector, 30 per cent from universities and 20 per cent from industry sector (Wood, 1982, p. 461) plays an important role in providing bibliographic and physical access to gray literature. NTIS has about 2.2 million bibliographic items in its stock and adds about 70,000 items every year.

6.2.2.1 *Bibliographic Control and Access :* By very nature, reports are neither easily accessible nor fully and satisfactorily subjected to bibliographic control. There are hundreds of organisations in each field bringing out thousands of reports each year. However, a small segment consisting of unclassified, declassified and unrestricted reports released for clearing houses and depositories are fairly bibliographically controlled. One can even say that they are subjected to excess bibliographic control leading to problems of overlapping coverage in announcement bulletins, multiplicity of report accession numbers and duplication of efforts. One source makes a safe estimate that at least 90 per cent of the unclassified report literature on aerospace and its allied technologies are covered in abstracting services (Macadam, 1973, p. 50).

A derogatory thing for libraries in India is that one pays hard foreign exchange to subscribe to many announcement bulletins such as STAR, GRA&I, etc., which overlap in their coverage to a great extent. As number of announcement bulletins subscribed by the Library is increased the law of diminishing return operates rigorously giving very few new relevant reports. On the other hand not having sufficient announcement bulletins hinders the process of identifying correct bibliographic details before approaching the right source for supply.

Table 6.1 presents a selected list of announcement bulletins and sources for reports. Some of the announcement bulletins are quite complicated for use. Leave alone the innocent users, even trained library staff have to spend sufficient time to study and familiarise the classification and arrangement of entries, codes, symbols, etc., used in different announcement bulletins. As an illustration one can examine STAR and GRA&I. All reports listed in STAR are not available for purchase. Even those available have to be purchased from USGPO or NTIS. Though STAR uses many codes and symbols, its arrangement and subject orientation are much better than GRA&I.

TABLE 6.1: Selected Announcement Bulletins and Sources for Reports

Sl. No.	Title	Publisher	Country	Periodicity	Approx. no. of reports per yr.	Source for procurement
1.	GRA&I	NTIS	USA	BW	70,000	NTIS
2.	ERA	DOE	USA	SM	27,000	USGPO & NTIS
3.	STAR	NASA	USA	SM	25,000	USGOP & NTIS
4.	TAB	DDC	USA	SM	40,000	(Classified & restricted)
5.	Monthly Catalog	USGPO	USA	M	NA	USGPO
6.	SRA	The Rand Corp.	USA	Q	400	The Rand Corp.
7.	Catalog of ESA Pub.	ESA	UK	A	150	ESA
8.	R&D Abstract (Ceased)	TRC	UK	SM	6,000	TRC
9.	BRTT*	BLLD	UK	M	4,000	BLLD

Key: * It is claimed that about a lakh reports are acquired per year by BLLD (Wood, 1982, p. 400).

On the other hand, NTIS, the biggest self-sustaining commercial source for reports, does not restrict to any subject or field. As a result GRA&I (one of its many dissemination tools) not only covers reports on virtually almost all fields without any quality checks but also overlaps in coverage with other lists and services of NTIS as well as STAR. NTIS has adopted both COSATI subject categories and subject categories of its own for arrangement of entries and items in GRA&I, SRIM and other dissemination services. Subject index of GRA&I is further complicated by lack of controlled vocabulary and use of four major and five minor thesauri defeating the very purpose of using controlled vocabulary. This is precisely because three organisations namely DDC, DOE and NASA provide their inputs to NTIS after processing with their respective thesauri. Other reports are indexed by NTIS using TEST apart from use of additional minor thesauri wherever needed. The argument of NTIS to shift the burden of multiple thesauri on users is not convincing. In addition to such incompatibilities, GRA&I is strongly criticised by many users for its arrangement, too broad and unpredictable coverage, delay in publishing indexes, especially annual indexes, overlapping with the coverage of other announcement bulletins, inconsistent bibliographic entries, announcing reports which are not distributed by NTIS, multiplicity of report numbers and too many cross referencing entries in between primary entries. Thus GRA&I is a typical 'Kitchidi' mixing up everything and making its productive use for selection and procurement of reports limited.

Many organisations within USA as well as outside USA have no binding to distribute their reports only through NTIS or similar agencies. As a result good number of reports available from NTIS are also available directly from originating organisations at a much cheaper price. Most of the non-US reports (including RAE, DFVLR, AGARD, etc.) and few US reports such as Rand Corporation, JPL, etc., could be cited as examples.

In spite of these handicaps and soaring prices of its products, NTIS has been growing strong. For libraries in India, NTIS has become almost inevitable source for buying many reports as India neither has a national clearing house/depository for reports nor direct access to major US organisations such as NASA, DDC, DOE, etc.

6.2.2.2 *Avoiding Duplication* : Once decided to buy reports a precarious problem of duplication of their contents with other forms of literature already available or likely to be procured shortly is faced. "It is generally believed that much of the material presented in technical reports is often republished in other forms such as journal articles" (Ary and Saul, 1959). It is further indicated in the study that 50 per cent of AFOSR and 60 per cent of NASA classified reports are eventually published in open literature and about one third of all unclassified technical reports of USAEC (in 1958) were published as articles in professional or technical periodicals. Another survey (Dwighte and Staffen, 1957) of 2,500 unclassified technical reports by

Library of Congress showed that about 60-65 per cent of reports contain publishable information, about half of which are published in the open literature within 2-3 years, a fifth of such reports are not published for several years. Thus "an appreciable fraction of information in technical reports appear within a year or two in conventionally published form" (National Academy of Science and National Academy of Engineering, 1969, p. 116) although there may not be one-to-one relation between report and article or conference paper. It was found very difficult to avoid this sort of content duplication (which is normally not noticed till the incidence of use) between reports and periodical articles, conference papers and occasionally, monographs.

Another type of duplication is by acquiring two or more copies of the same report. This may occur as one copy might have been received as gift or on exchange basis or as part of a standing order and the other is purchased against demand during the same period. Library has very little control over such situation unless on demand purchase is initiated after a month or two of receiving first copy. Such duplication may also occur due to different report numbers/contract numbers/report accession numbers, as reports are normally checked for duplication by their primary report number rather than author and title. Normally, suppliers insist on report accession number allotted by them than the primary number for quick supply. However, users continue to quote primary report number or contract number. This problem is an extension of bibliographic control aggravated by multiplicity of report numbers, discussed in greater detail later. The order trays, catalogues (card cabinet) and actual arrangement of reports depend heavily on report numbers, which are supposed to be unique (and hence called 'pseudo call numbers'), for avoiding duplicates as well as retrieval. That means order trays and catalogues should provide approach to all possible report numbers including contract numbers and accession numbers of report handling agencies such as NASA and NTIS. In addition, the unintelligible multiplicity of numbers may arise due to multiple sponsorship, contract numbers, grant numbers and accession numbers of the successive handling agencies. The advantages, if any, of contract numbers, grant numbers and accession numbers of handling agencies is offset by need to create too many cross references and resultant irritating and bulky card catalogues and order trays. Further, accession numbers added by less popular agencies who neither have comprehensive coverage nor announcement bulletins are nuisance. Many reports contain some report numbers printed and others handwritten, often incomplete and leading to difficulty in recognising and providing cross references in card catalogues and order trays. Ambiguous presentation of report number is also not uncommon. The problem of unintentionally landing up with a duplicate copy of report can be avoided to some extent if one or two unambiguous, permanent, complete, concise and unique report numbers are used in a consistent way with each and every report.

6.2.2.3 *Efficiency and Effectiveness of Suppliers* : Choosing appropriate efficient and effective supplier/vendor for timely and regular supply of reports is necessary. Unlike books, choosing right vendor for reports is always complicated and difficult. As already mentioned there are a number of report originating agencies such as ESA, RAE, FSI, Rand Corporation, UOW, DFVLR, etc., which supply reports directly. Several agencies such as NTIS, INFODOC, INFONORME, USGPO, BLLD, HMSO, etc. act as commercial sources with widely differing price schedules. The price schedule of agencies such as NTIS are highly differentiated between foreign and domestic and other allied countries. The economy aspect of buying is dealt in detail in a later section. All except NTIS could be approached directly or through any vendor. NTIS has three exclusive agents in India with identical price schedule and other conditions.

To assess the efficiency and effectiveness of all these suppliers is very difficult as it involves many factors apart from economy. First of all non-supply of reports for years is quite derogatory. Status of pending supplies from a representative random sample orders made at ISAC Library is presented in Table 6.2. The first three suppliers in the table are official agents of NTIS in India. Fourth represent a group of foreign vendors. The fifth and sixth are mostly direct supply sources i.e., report originating agencies. The following limitations of the data should be noted before drawing any inference. Firstly, most of the orders on Indian agents were made during 1980 and 81 whereas almost all orders on Foreign agents and suppliers were made during 1981 and 1982. Secondly, all the three Indian agents of NTIS supply reports by mandatory air freight at extra cost of $1.65 and $3.00 (1982) per report depending on volume of report. On the other hand, all orders made on foreign suppliers were for sea mail supply and some of them insist on advance payment till our volume of order crosses a minimum level to allow credit system. Both the reasons lead to some delay in supply of reports in case of foreign suppliers.

Now, looking at Table 6.2, it is very clear that the over-all effectiveness of supply position, as far as pending supplies are concerned, is not at all encouraging. Among the three Indian agents of NTIS, Agent 2 has fared slightly better than the other two. A real comparison between Indian agents and Foreign suppliers should also take into account efficiency and economy. Ignoring all limitations, one can see that direct supply sources and Indian agents are slightly better in their effectiveness.

TABLE 6.2: Pending Supplies of Reports for Selected Orders (made during 1 April 1980 and 30 September 1982 and as on 31 December 1982)

Sl. No.	Supplier	No. of Reps. ordered	No. of Reps. Pending	% of Reps. Pending
1.	NTIS Agent 1	50	8	16
2.	NTIS Agent 2	198	10	5
3.	NTIS Agent 3	25	3	2
4.	Foreign Agents	355	88	25
5.	ESA	150	36	24
6.	Others (DFVLR, FSI, ISRG, etc.)	29	4	14
	Total	807	149	18

The efficiency aspect of suppliers, i.e., how soon reports are supplied, is presented in Table 6.3 for random sample orders made during April 1981.Here again, one has to note that it takes 3-4 months to receive reports by sea mail in case of foreign suppliers. The following inferences can be drawn from the table subject to limitations noted earlier. Direct supply from report originating agencies (Sl. Nos. 5 & 6 in Table 6.3) is not only fast but almost complete by the end of nine months. Only about 50 per cent of the items were supplied by Indian agents within three months. That is in case of half of the items the very purpose of paying extra mandatory air freight charges is defeated. It may be noted that Indian agents promise to supply reports within 8-10 weeks. Among Indian agents of

NTIS, Agent 2 and Agent 3 have supplied 84 per cent and 87 per cent of reports respectively within six months, though they have pending supplies of 6 per cent and 13 per cent respectively at the end of one year. The supply has almost stopped at the end of six months in the case of Agent 1 and Agent 3 while it continued in a diminishing rate in the case of Agent 2. The supply has reached peak during 6-9 months period in the case of foreign agents and later continued in diminishing rate. Obviously there is no supply of reports within three months in case of foreign agents. However, by giving a grace of 3-4 months or by switching over to airmail supply, foreign agents are almost on par with Indian agents in their efficiency.

TABLE 6.3: Efficiency of Suppliers of Reports

Sl. No.	Supplier	No. of Reps. ordered	Percentage of Reports supplied Within 3 m	Within 3-6 m	Within 6-9 m	Within 9-12 m	% of Reps. Pending at end of yr.
1.	NTIS Agent 1	49	33	50	0	0	17
2.	NTIS Agent 2	94	50	34	9	1	6
3.	NTIS Agent 3	24	54	33	0	0	13
4.	Foreign Agents	181	0	25	48	4	23
5.	ESA	55	45	40	0	0	15
6.	Others (DFVLR, FSI, ISRG, etc.)	27	63	33	0	0	4
	Total	430	27	33	22	2	16

To sum up, the process of choosing an appropriate vendor/ supplier for reports is to be based on: (i) economy, which will be discussed shortly, (ii) efficiency as reflected in supply position experienced by the library, (iii) effectiveness and (iv) informativeness and readiness of suppliers to respond to queries of the library in addition to other criteria discussed in Chapter 4 (4.3.2). The fourth consideration is qualitative involving value judgment and the risk of subjectivity. Also this criterion is not normally applicable to foreign agents and direct supply sources as they give less attention to such correspondence. Indian libraries being located far away from major agencies such as NTIS (whose service cannot be availed without sufficient clarifications), one is forced to depend on Indian agents for any clarification or information.

6.2.2.4 *Problems of Economy :* Number of relevant reports in a field may increase by about 10 per cent and the price by about 10 to 20 per cent per year. As marginally increased budget cannot balance these two changes and other factors discussed in Chapter 4 (4.3.10), the buying power of a library steadily decreases unless greater attention is paid to explore opportunities and find out avenues to buy more information at essentially same or little increased price. Hence, any library has to care to study the economies of procurement, which obviously has enough scope.

Unlike books, reports are not uniformly priced nor always copyrighted. Further, reports are available from multiple sources with different prices in different currencies and often in cheap microfiche form. Thus, by looking at these apparent facts of the situation one can try to substitute microforms wherever possible, explore the possibility of resource sharing, intensify requests for free copies and copies on exchange basis, look for alternate cheaper sources and even go in for xeroxing reports which are not copyrighted.

As pointed out earlier, ideal is to grab the report from originating organisations at right time either as gift or on exchange basis. When one inevitably resorts to buying a report one has to consider economy of the source of supply apart from efficiency, effectiveness and other considerations. To pinpoint how the prices vary among different suppliers, a comparison of selected price schedules of suppliers of reports (as of 1982) is presented in Table 6.4. The table excludes exceptionally priced items, standing orders and microforms.

One may note that differentiated pricing is followed by most of the agencies. For example, NTIS charges for Indian customers is double the domestic charges applicable to customers in US and USAID countries. Similarly, USGPO charges additional 25 per cent to overseas customers and ESA levies 20 per cent surcharge on buyers from non-member states. USGPO allows even overseas customers to maintain deposit account and luckily does not have Indian agents in between. In case of ESA, the price schedule is applicable to original printed reports and whenever original printed reports are not available and microfiche copies are not opted, xerox copies are supplied as per separate price schedule.

TABLE 6.4: Comparison of Selected Price Schedules of Suppliers of Reports (1982)

No. of pages	NTIS Foreign ($)	NTIS Domestic ($)	Micro-media (C$)	GED ($)	BLLD (P)	ESA Foreign ($)	ESA Member (FF)	Rand Corpn. ($)
1	12	6	8.45 + 1.50	($3 + 22c per p)	(1.97 per 10p)			
20								
25				8.50				3
40	15	7.50	13.55 + 3.00		7.88			
50				14.00		15	60	
60	18	9			11.82			5
75			25.35 + 6.00	19.50				
80	21	10.50						
100				25	19.70			
	24	12						
125			33.75 + 9.00	30.50				
	27	13.50				22		7
150				36	29.55		90	
	30	15						
175			42.15 + 12.00	41.50				
	33	16.50						
200				47	39.40			
201-500	3 per 25p	1.50 per 25p	0.25 per p	22 c per p	1.97 per 10p	34	140	10
>500	3 per 25p	1.50 per 25p	0.25 per p	22 c per p	1.97 per 10p	44	175	10
Photocopies						0.40 per p +	2 per p	
Freight	1.65/$3		$3					

It can be seen from Table 6.4 that an average report of 200 pages costs $33 plus $3 towards mandatory air freight charges through an Indian agent of NTIS. If the same report is bought from other sources up to 50 per cent can be saved depending on the nature of report and the source. Since the pricing is based on number of pages, selection of source has to be based on the volume of the report. As far as possible, reports should be bought from the originating agencies. This will be obvious if we compare the price structure of the Rand Corporation with that of NTIS. BLLD price structure is basically meant for supply of photocopies of periodical articles and it may be economical only for a very short report. It is also learnt that the BLLD and Microinfo, the official agents of NTIS in U.K., are working closely to establish a revised price structure for NTIS services (Wood, 1982, p. 460) in UK. On the other hand, GED and to some extent Micromedia Ltd. are cheaper than NTIS for reports less than 100 pages. One should also note that "NTIS reports are also available from other libraries and documentation centres that have purchased stocks" (Vickers, 1982, p. 502).

Lastly, Table 6.5 presents the average landed cost of reports from different sources based on a large sampling study of procurement at ISAC Library during 1982. It is crystal clear from the table that direct purchase costs less than half the cost through an Indian agent and roughly two-thirds the cost through a foreign agent. Similarly, the average cost of a report bought from a foreign agent is two-thirds of a report bought from an Indian agent. This average cost is worked out ignoring the reports received as free and on exchange basis.

From the above observations, it may be concluded that by and large, as far as possible, one should avoid sources and agencies which are gigantic and commercial in nature with heavy overhead costs and also those having agents and sub-agents.

TABLE 6.5: Average Landed Cost of Paper Copy Reports from Different Sources (1982)

Sl.No.	Supplier	Cost (Rs.)
1.	Indian Agents	254
2.	Foreign Agents	171
3.	Other Direct Sources	111

6.2.2.5 *Problems Relating to Physical Condition of Reports :* Except where reports are directly received from originating agencies, all other sources supply either xerox copies or copies reproduced from microfiche originals leading to poor physical appearance and illegible prints, diagrams and photographs. Loose sheets of reports are stapled together or adhesive bound with or without a thin wrapper. Such reports are normally two times bulkier than original due to reproduction on one side of the paper and do not stand freely on library shelves nor they can withstand constant use by readers. As such a delay of minimum of one month has to be added to such supply before releasing them to use due to compulsory binding work involved. However small in-house bindery may reduce delay to some extent. Further, it is often noticed that due to insufficient margins and non-uniform reproduction, binding work is made more difficult and clear readability of bound report is affected.

Even though NTIS claims that approximately one in five chances customers receive hard-bound printed reports, such chances are very rare in highly specialised subjects having relatively less demand on NTIS. Mostly stapled or wax-bound poorly reproduced reports, often with a note that the reproduction is poor as the original report itself was not clear and legible, are supplied. This is a common feature even in microfiche reports.

6.2.2.6 *Problems of Report Numbers :* The most important and probably the unique characteristic of reports is their alphanumeric designations called Report Series Code Numbers or simply Report Numbers. Report Code is that portion of report number which designates the issuing or controlling agency. The accession or handling number and contract or grant or project number are often deemed to be report numbers for the purpose of identifying and handling reports but they are handicaps in many respects. Even report numbers themselves pose many problems due to lack of consistency in their creation and use. However, owing to their simplicity, brevity and mnemonic value, report numbers have gained popularity as security codes, filing designators and bibliographic references. Physical and bibliographic identification, access, control and organisation are very much aided by these 'pseudo call numbers' of reports. Report number is not only an example of a suitable substitute for source classification but also remains as a challenge to classification in its popularity. It also serves as an example where universally accepted practice of subject arrangement and browsing of documents are sacrificed for ease of handling as report numbers rarely represent subjects. Thus even today most of the technical reports in many libraries escape rigorous ritual of subject classification based on standard schemes of classification.

Many reports are produced as per standard and contain a full page 'document control data sheet', perforated ready-to-use source index cards with full bibliographic details, abstract and sometimes even UDC class numbers.

Most of the problems of report numbers are rooted in excessive practice of their flexible merits. There is no uniformity in what basically a report code should represent. Many times, report numbers are made to represent issuing or contracting or distributing agency and/or its subordinate agency, individual author, subject, form, date of issue, security code, short title, etc. of the report depending on whims and fancies of issuing agencies. The uncontrolled proliferation of report numbering schemes, mainly due to increased number of reports, lack of enforcement of standards and control measures, mushrooming of report handling agencies and their announcement bulletins, have made the report numbers complicated and unintelligible. Further, ambiguous presentation of report numbers is quite common. Inconsistent way of permuting the components of report numbers and connecting symbols such as hyphen, colon and dot can be found in many reports. Those who have treated connecting symbols as sacred tools of classification will have to be consoled while taking a look at how connecting symbols are treated in report numbers. Most of the connecting symbols of report numbers play no role in filing order. It would be amusing and interesting if some one takes up a detailed comparison of report numbers with classification numbers of any scheme. However, there are some clear similarities between report numbers and book numbers. An unwanted similarity of report numbers and class numbers is that when report numbers are changed, instructions are issued (though very rarely) for renumbering all reports issued earlier. Change of name of issuing agency, decision to add or modify series and connecting symbols result in inconsistent report numbers.

Another equally strong hazard is use of multiple numbers to identify a single report. This multiplicity of numbers due to multiple sponsorship as well as additional numbers in the form of contract number, grant number, accession number, etc., make the situation worse. It is very commonly seen that most of the reports carry three or four report numbers. Many reports contain some numbers printed and others hand-written, often incomplete and illegible. An example of a single report bearing seven different numbers is quoted in *Dictionary of Report Series Code*. This dictionary had 13,000 codes in its first edition (1973). To quote from the introduction of this dictionary (Godfrey and Redman, 1973, p. 4): "Hundreds of agencies were involved in [report number] assignment and use; thousands of different codes in different forms sprang up. There was no way to control them. There was, and is, no way to assess their reliability. Some codes are well-known and indicate the source of the reports, while others mean nothing. Yet all have been used indiscriminately for reference and control". Successive handling agencies dealing with reports either modify the existing number or add new ones contributing to the complications.

The problems of bibliographic control of technical reports is very much aggravated by multiplicity of report numbers including contract numbers and accession numbers. Further, agencies such as NTIS insist on quoting their accession numbers while ordering reports for 'quick supply', while users continue to quote original report number such as NASA numbers. A library is likely to land up with multiple copies of the same report at exorbitant cost unless provision is made in card index and order trays for access through all types of numbers used for a report. Thus even the accession numbers, distributing codes and contract or grant numbers which not only occupy a lot of space in bibliographic tools but also of least use outside the originating agencies have attained the stature of report series code numbers. Filing reports by report accession numbers is disastrous except where reports are exclusively received from one or two agencies. The advantages of report accession numbers is offset by the need to create cross references as explained above, and resultant irritating and bulky catalogues and order trays. In addition, accession numbers added by less popular agencies who neither have comprehensive coverage nor announcement bulletins can be hazardous. Often report numbers are quite lengthy. One can see many reports bearing numbers with 20 or more characters. Report numbers are further proliferated by abundance of errors in texts and announcement bulletins. There are a number of cases where same report is issued under different numbers as well as different reports carrying identical report number. Again, *Dictionary of Report Series Codes* shows how AFOSR Reports in a single GRA&I issue are listed in seven different ways.

Lastly, report codes do have plenty of synonyms. IR stands for eleven different meanings. NAL stands for both National Aeronautical Laboratory of India and National Aerospace Laboratory of Japan. These are only a few of the examples.

6.2.2.7 *Problems of Security Classification of Reports :* Apart from not having access to many reports of totalitarian countries (except a few released and translated for the consumption of outsiders) one is kept in dark about majority of reports produced in even democratic countries like U.S.A. and U.K. because of military or otherwise security classification and limited circulation restrictions imposed. It is claimed that reports are security classified due to sensitive information of national importance contained in them.

It appears that automatic time bound declassification of classified reports does not take place in some countries. Further reports of R&D units of industries cannot be made available to public on strategic grounds till at least patents are established. In these areas even if the concept is in embryonic stage, a third party knowing it is denied.

Information whose disclosure to unauthorised persons could jeopardize national security is termed 'classified material'. According to U.S. law, there are three levels or categories of classification, namely 'top secret', 'secret' and 'confidential'. Another special category called 'restricted data' which is born classified as per law is applicable to atomic energy information. The term 'official use only' is not a security classification but restricts access to administrative and other non-security purposes (Kent and Lancour, p. 174 & 177). There are about sixty markings ranging from 'addressee only' to 'top secret'.

Till World War II there were very few classified reports. But now classified reports may be much more than unclassified and declassified reports. It is estimated that there are 20 million classified documents with DOD (U.S.) with 31000 authorised individuals to exercise original classification and more than 100 classification managers. CSTAR of NASA covered about 90,000 classified and limited distribution documents during 1962-1972 and 90 per cent of CSTAR (now LSTAR) is from DOD (NASA, STIO, n.d.). Further, the National Archives (U.S.) holds 460 million pages of classified documents, USAEC excluding its contractors holds 8 million classified documents and (U.S.) Department of State holds 150 million documents. To review and declassify these documents it needs 10 years at $ 300,000 per year. The cost of even maintaining inventories of classified information is very high (Auger, 1975, p. 18). Further, hundred thousands of people are involved in derivative classification by which a citation or reference to a classified document will be considered as a new classified document. There are 13,000 security cleared contractors and their thousands of security cleared employees (approximately one million people) regularly assigning original or derivative classification to reports (Klempner, 1973, p. 262-264).

Though many classified and limited distribution reports are listed in confidential or classified announcement bulletins like *LSTAR* (formerly CSTAR) of NASA, *Technical Abstract Bulletin of DOD* and *USAEC Index of Limited Distribution Reports*, access to classified information and documents are strictly controlled. Those who establish need to know and obtain security clearance are only allowed to use (Kent and Lancour, p. 179 & 181). Accessing and obtaining classified report of a different country may either meet with negative reply or cause enormous delay. Foreign requests need to be routed through the embassies of both countries and success depends on the bilateral political relations of the countries involved apart from the nature of information contained in the report.

Certain obligations and responsibilities have to be fulfilled by libraries acquiring classified reports. Apart from careful handling of such reports, marking on such reports, restricting them from free lending, recording their movements, using code instead of full bibliographic details, stacking in closed access, etc., as stipulated in law, agreement or policy of the institution are necessary.

Periodic reviews of classified reports are supposed to be made by issuing or controlling agencies to declassify and make reports unlimited for distribution purpose or to lower the level of classification. About 10 per cent of NTIS's input consists of reports formerly classified or restricted (Thott, 1974, p. 42).

The very philosophy of security classification of reports (other than administrative, diplomatic and military reports) in democratic countries is criticised for thwarting and denying information by excessive classification restrictions and overzealous application of the concept of 'national security', negative or blank bibliographic control and delays and high costs involved in acquiring classified reports (Klempner, p. 268; Crowers, 1974, p. 1; Taylor, 1973, p. 195). Though it is claimed that classified information may remain secured for about 5 years or so (probably enemies may acquire them much earlier than scientists and engineers of one's own country), the security classification establishes barriers between nations, creates areas of uncertainty in the minds of public, impedes flow of useful information within one's own country and abroad, lead to under-utilisation of S&T capabilities, duplication of efforts, reluctance of young scientists to work on such areas and increase in 'invisible college' activities (Klempner, p. 264-265). The trend appears to be adopting over-classification with an eye on enactment of law to prevent publication of anything considered threatening to 'national interest' leading to confrontation between national security and science (*Newsweek*, 1982, p. 8-9). In addition to language and political barriers the security-classification is yet another big stumbling block in S&T information transfer through reports. Thus reports are not only gray or shadow literature but also dark literature when they are subjected to classification.

6.2.2.8 *Problems of Development of Internal Reports Collection* : Enormous information and data are generated in R&D organisations in their normal course of work. Such information in the form of technical reports, pre-prints, reprints, design drawings, manuals, etc., need to be acquired by a special library. The success of a special library partly depends on its ability to provide internally generated information. "Lack of internal documents is the most serious fate that can be fall an information service, because it cuts out the most important information, which no amount of published material can replace" (Hartas, 1967, p. 82). Nevertheless tendency to collect all internal reports including ad hoc, interim and administrative reports of ephemeral nature should be avoided.

A special library of an R&D organisation should automatically be a depository of internal reports. Due care should be taken in processing and organising internal classified and limited distribution reports. A comprehensive collection of internal reports helps in avoiding duplication of efforts. Distribution of such reports through library enables the library to settle amicably the exchange agreements with outside organisations and saves lot of funds that too foreign exchange. Many R&D organisations abroad offer their reports on exchange basis.

Often libraries are not able to get all internal reports prepared in the organisations due to negligence of report originating department, lack of centralisation of production of reports, lack of policy of production and distribution of reports, underestimation of importance of internal reports, lack of coordination and total lack of (or overemphasis on) security and lack of screening mechanism within the organisation. However, libraries should strive to get into the distribution list of each and every report.

7

MICROFORMS COLLECTION

An attempt to quantify information explosion revealed that scientific information available at the time of Thomas Edison (1847-1931) could be represented in a bar chart with a 4″ high bar and the growth from the end of Second World War (1939-45) to 1967 presented on the same scale led to a bar as high as 70 storey building (Smith, 1978). Do we really have enough media to record, duplicate and distribute these tremendous information out put? Of the three media, viz., paper, electronic storage and microfilm, the electronic storage is still quite costly and paper has become dearer in almost all countries. Taking for granted that enough paper is available, it would be a herculean task for any library to acquire, organise and retrieve all relevant information in paper medium alone. This is how inevitably microforms have entered the fray. More and more libraries are acquiring microforms to overcome their budget cuts and inflation, to avoid unlimited extension of library stacks, to maximise acquisition of relevant information with their inelastic budgets, to cut delays in acquiring information and to achieve ease in handling and storage. Surprisingly, the aggressive selling strategies of trade have also contributed considerably in promoting microforms. This is in spite of the fact that users always, and almost everywhere, resisted use of microforms.

Now-a-days many manuals of equipment and R&D reports are available only in microforms. This does not mean that microforms are bought in libraries unwillingly and without advantages. In fact, microforms are modern, efficient and powerful communication and information-handling tools affording enough opportunities and threats to librarian. They have vital role to play in providing information services if actively adopted as a 'system' giving due consideration for user reactions and supporting facilities. A library can either convert its existing collection to microform through its own microfilming facility or through job worker or acquire microforms from outside agencies and micropublishers.

Collection development policy of a special library should spell out level of investment to be made on microforms, preferred physical types and formats of microforms and other technical criteria. "An inventory of microform equipment already owned by the library is a useful first step in formulating a policy for microform selection" (Eichorn, 1985, p. 350). Such inventory helps in discarding unsuitable items and building microforms collection compatible to user-aid facility.

7.1 Types of Microforms

Microform is one which carry almost permanently reduced images of printed or written matter in such a way that the reduced images are no longer legible to read with naked eye. Microforms are compact, uniform, light weight, versatile, clean and inexpensive information storing and handling media (Smith, 1978). Microform is a generic term for any form, either film or paper, which contains micro-images. Before examining the role of microforms in collection development, a quick look at the basics of micrographics may be necessary.

Miniaturised printing is most primitive type of microform wherein images are printed at about 5X reduction ratio (Williams, 1975). Normally miniaturised printing is adopted for publishing reference works such as dictionaries and encyclopedias and a magnifying lens is provided with each copy.

7.1.1 *Micro Opaque Cards*

Micro opaque cards are flat rectangular opaque material on which one or more images are recorded. Reading of opaque card is based on light reflection principle. The size of micro-cards vary from 3″ X 5″ to 6″ X 9″. R&D reports were regularly brought out in this form. Even though opaque cards have the advantage of recording images on both sides, they have almost ceased quite some time ago giving way to newer forms.

7.1.2 *Microfilm*

Open reel film is one of the earliest microforms extensively used for archival purpose. The width of a film could be 16 mm, 35mm, 70mm, or 105 mm, and length normally around 100 feet. In addition to spool or open reel, microfilms are also available in cartridges and cassettes. Newspapers, back volumes of periodicals and books are available in microfilm. Microfilm offers only sequential and hence comparatively slow access to information.

7.1.3 *Microfilm Jackets or Unitised Microfilm*

Microfilm jackets are transparent plastic carriers with single or multiple sleeves or pockets made to hold microfilm in flat strips (NMA, 1976). Jackets could be 3″ X 5″ or 4″ X 6″ or 5″ X 8″ and microfilm strips could be 16 mm or 35 mm wide. Periodical articles and other shorter documents are normally produced in this form. Microfilm jackets have greatest advantage of acting as master for producing microfiches and allowing for easy updating. Of late microfilm jackets are also available in the form of continuous stationery mounted on sprocketed computer stationery.

7.1.4 *Microfiche*

Microfiche is a sheet of microfilm containing multiple micro-images in a grid pattern (NMA, 1976). It usually contains a title which can be read without magnifying aid. Microfiches are available in various sizes such as 3″ X 5″, 4″ X 6″, 8.5″ X 11.5″, etc., with different reduction ratios. The most common size of microfiche is A6 (i.e., 4″ X 6″) and common reduction ratios are 24X, 42X, 48X and 60X. The number of image frames vary from 60 to 200 depending on the size and reduction ratio. For example, a 24X microfiche of A6 size will have 98 frames. A6 size microfiche can be made by cutting 105 mm microfilm roll at every 6″. Normally, reports, individual issues and papers of periodicals, conference papers, books and monographs are available in microfiche. Microfiche allows for random access to information and it is extremely cheap to duplicate a microfiche. For instance, a 98-frame microfiche costs about Rs. 10 to duplicate. As such microfiche has become an extremely popular medium among microforms.

7.1.5 *Ultramicrofiche or PCMI (Photo Chromic Micro Images)*

Ultramicrofiche is a microfiche with high reduction ratio, i.e., reduction exceeding 90X. Ultramicrofiches are recorded via two-stage reduction with sophisticated techniques and stringent environmental control. It will have reduction ratio up to 150X and number of image frames up to 3200 on a sheet. Ultramicrofiches are yet to become popular due to sophistication involved. National Cash Register Company has marketed some ultramicrofiches. "Books in English" of BNB was brought out in ultramicrofiche (Williams, 1975).

7.1.6 *Aperture Cards*

Aperture cards are standard Hollerith cards or edge-notched cards with a die-cut rectangular hole or aperture for the purpose of holding one or more frames of flat microfilm. Aperture cards lend to easy indexing and mechanisation. They are best suited for engineering drawings and patents. The aperture size is normally 35X48 mm which can hold one 35 mm or two 16mm frames. However, an 'eight up' version of aperture card can hold eight A4/quarto size frames at 24X reduction in 35 mm film. In recent days not only aperture cards are made to hold two or more rows or columns of 16 mm or 35 mm film strips but also aperture cards of standard microfiche (6″X4″) size are brought out with different size apertures.

7.1.7 *Computer Output Microfilm (COM)*

Computer Output Microfilm (COM) is a microfilm containing data produced by a recorder (COM device) from computer generated electrical signals. In this process digital data stored on magnetic media is directly converted by computer into human readable language on microfilm. COM is very promising, exciting and it eliminates the concept of original paper copy of the document. However, it is limited to computerised information (Smith, 1978).

7.2 Micrographics Terms and Concepts

7.2.1 *Opaque and Translucent*

A microform could be opaque or translucent. All microforms which do not allow light to pass through are opaque. A translucent microform does partially allow light to pass through. Except micro-opaque card and miniaturised printing all other microforms explained above are translucents. While translucents are read on readers by light refraction principle, micro-opaque card readers adopt light reflection principle. Opaque forms have an advantage of recording information on both sides.

7.2.2 *Base and Emulsion*

Translucent microforms usually have an acetate, triacetate or polyester transparent base on which is uniformly coated a thin layer (= 0.0005″) of light sensitive chemical called photographic emulsion. Normally, film itself is called either silver-halide or diazo or vesicular/kalvar depending on emulsion layer coated on base. Table 7.1 indicates certain qualities, advantages and disadvantages of these types of films.

TABLE 7.1: Comparative Assessment of Different Films (Emulsions)

	Silver halide	Vesicular/ Kalvar	Diazo
1. Cost	Most expensive	Midway	Cheap
2. Application	Used for original preparation	Used for duplicate copies	Used for duplicate copies
3. Process	Complex and Wet	Fairly easy	Easy
4. Light sensitivity	Sensitive to white light	Sensitive to ultraviolet light	Sensitive to ultraviolet light
5. Archival quality	Indefinite	Midway	Comparatively limited (affected by continuous exposure to light)
6. Resistance to wear & tear	Moderate	Midway	Good
7. Polarity on copying	Reversible	Reversible as well as non-reversible	Non-reversible

7.2.3 *Polarity*

Microforms can be either positive or negative. A positive or dark line image is one which has black prints on a light background and the negative or clear line image has background with prints as clear light piercing transparent area. Both positive as well as negative films have certain advantages. Important merits of both are given in Table 7.2.

In practice negative films have become more popular than positive mainly due to cheap diazo reproduction of negative film from a master negative.

TABLE 7.2: Merits of Positive and Negative Films

Positive Film	Negative Film
1. Psychological acquaintance of users	Conceals or masks dirt, scratches, dust, etc., on film
2. Requires lower level of illumination	Lesser eye strain
3. Sharp image suitable for high ambient illumination	Tolerates slight defects in screen
4. More contrast in the image	Acts as original for cheap diazo duplication
5. Clear tonal illustrations	Some reader printers are available only for negative films

7.2.4 *Reduction and Enlargement Ratios*

Reduction is a measure of the number of times a given dimension of an object is reduced when photographed (NMA, 1974). It is expressed as 24X or "24 to 1." This means that the original image was reduced to an image 1/24th as high and 1/24th as wide. Since the reduction is two-dimensional, the film image occupies only 1/576th (1/24 X 24th) as much space as did the original image (Smith, 1978). There are various ranges of reduction ratios designed to accommodate different size originals and different number of frames.

Enlargement is the reverse of reduction and it is reproduction larger than the original or the intermediate.

7.2.5 *Density*

Density refers to the amount of light which is stopped or allowed to pass through the film. For a negative film, background density is measured in the black background areas of the film and line density is measured in the clear area (Smith, 1978).

7.2.6 *Resolution*

Resolving power is a photographic term and it refers to the degree to which a lens, optical system or film emulsion is able to define the details of an image, expressed as the number of lines per millimetre, discernible in an image (NMA, 1974).

7.2.7 *Generation*

Generation is a measure of the remoteness of a particular copy from the original material. The first negative copy made from original is called first generation negative microfilm (i.e., 1N). Copies made from 1N are either second generation positive microfilm (i.e., 2P) or second generation negative microfilm (i.e., 2N) and so on (NMA, 1974).

7.3 Roles and Advantages of Microforms

7.3.1 *Microforms as Economical Media*

The first and most important role of microform is reduction in library expenditure for acquiring same amount of information. Cost reduction is direct in purchase price of microform as well as indirect in the form of postage, handling, storage, retrieval, etc. The price reduction of microform versions of published documents varies from 10 to 95 per cent depending on format and reduction ratio of microform and the market demand for the documents in microform. This role of microform is considered as an important factor in these days of budget cuts, inflation, high postal charges and soaring printing and paper costs. The case study of reports-collection-development at ISAC library presented in previous chapter showed the tremendous saving of over 90 per cent on purchase price without sacrificing any relevant information. Further, all microfiche reports were received by air freight, without additional airfreight and handling charges and much earlier than receipt of reports announcement bulletins.

The economy of microforms is very high and in this context experts opine that duplication of microform is becoming so cheap that it would be possible to give microform copies of documents to readers at a throw-away price in near future (if copyright restrictions are overcome) instead of issuing a paper copy for a short period.

However, microforms do require additional expenditure on maintenance, reading, enlarging and printing equipments.

7.3.2 *Microforms as Space Saving Devices*

Microforms require 90 to 98 per cent less space than that required by corresponding hard copies (Smith, 1978). However, actual saving might be little less depending on type and reduction ratio of microform, extent of supporting equipment facilities needed, etc.

Space is precious in many special libraries and it costs them to maintain each square feet. Libraries in metropolitan cities have long back resorted to microfilming their less used documents to conserve valuable space. Obviously, converting existing collection to microform and maintaining both hard copies and microforms may not save space, but on the other hand needs additional space.

About 70,000 microfiche reports are stored at ISAC library in about 50 sq. ft. area and the entire collection with reading and printing facilities is housed in less than 500 sq. ft. plinth area. Experts say that it is possible to store 1,75,000 titles of books/reports on 300 microfilm reels of 5″ diameter. Even in a library where space is easily and liberally available compact storage in manageable size is very much desired from the angle of easy access and maintenance.

7.3.3 *Microforms as Faster Carriers of Information*

Time is an important factor in providing information service that to in a special library. When a document has to be procured from abroad, one normally waits up to a minimum of four months to receive them by surface mail or else pays 50 to 150 per cent extra to receive paper copies by airmail. Microforms offer best solutions in such situations. Most of the suppliers mail microforms by airmail without additional handling and postage charges and the information is available within a month. Moreover, inland purchases through mail and inter-library transactions become not only cheap but also fast through microforms.

7.3.4 *Microforms as File Integrating Agents*

Any file should be complete and in proper sequence to have 'integrity' (Smith, 1978). The purpose of file is to provide all the information in its proper place, all the time, and microform does that extremely well. User can view a microform, duplicate it or take a paper copy. However, the original goes back to its place in the file to be ready for next use.

In addition, file integrity coupled with compact storage eliminates all problems connected with multivolume paper copies. NTIS retrospective index in microfiche is an example. A paper copy cumulative index can not be as compact and as comprehensive as microfiche Index (Author, Title and Report/Accession Number) which covers bibliographical details of 7 lakh R&D reports taken into NTIS collection during 1964 through 1978 in 1375 microfiche of 48X reduction each with 270 frames. This index greatly facilitates searching for 15 years period at a stretch.

7.3.5 *Microforms Facilitate Easy Mechanisation and Automation*

The simplest form of mechanisation involved is storing microforms in an electrically operated rotary files and retrieving relevant items mechanically. Several semiautomatic and fully automatic retrieval systems are also available in foreign markets. Aperture cards with their punched or edge notched coding lend themselves easily to mechanisation. In addition, various microform indexing techniques help handling and retrieval of relevant part of the microform quickly and efficiently. Modern microform readers and reader-printers possess such capabilities in varying degrees.

Mini and micro-computers entailing limited storage space and reasonable cost, in combination with compact data storage through microforms can offer a better information retrieval system known as 'on line access/off line retrieval'. In this system, it is envisaged that documents are stored in microform and index data are entered into computer. This is expected to save a lot of time and comes very close to a real time system. Alternatively, bibliographical data along with data regarding location of microform may be computerised, so that document back up service becomes faster at no extra cost.

It has already been noted that a microfiche can be generated directly from a computer terminal. This is expected to give great impetus to micropublishers. Once cost of storing information in computer is considerably reduced, automatic information retrieval system becomes cheap and easy through COM. Further, COM can virtually bring decentralisation of information by quickly providing document to the ultimate user wherever he is. The following estimates of experts about computers and COM should clear any doubt in one's mind about this 'difficult-to believe phenomenon'. It is said that computers are able to transfer digital data on microform at a rate of 1 lakh characters per second. COM device is considered to be 10 to 20 times faster than a line printer, 6 times less expensive than paper printout and 1/4th the expense of an on-line system.

7.3.6 *Microforms as Low Cost On-Demand Information Dissemination and Distribution Agents*

Since microforms can be easily, quickly, and inexpensively duplicated, information can be disseminated and distributed more effectively at less cost. As noted earlier a 98-page microfiche report can be instantaneously duplicated by diazo process for about Rs. 10.

Microforms are ideally suited for production, storage and distribution of internal reports of an R&D organisation. When a report is brought out, only a limited number of hard copies may be made for immediate distribution and a master negative fiche can be very easily and securely stored and duplicated as and when needed for distribution at future dates on exchange or gratis basis.

Microforms have helped publishers to bring short-run editions of books and monographs. This is how a lot of publishers including Pergamon Press and UMI are able to provide many out-of-print books in microform even when the demand is limited.

Further, there are a number of devices which transfer image from microform to printing plate by projecting microform image directly on offset master (Smith, 1978). This device coupled with COM device can give excellent and fast reproduction of copies and updating of any material.

7.3.7 *Microforms for Archival Value, Security of Information and Protection of Records*

Microforms properly processed and developed will have several hundred years of life. Since information on microform is difficult to alter or falsify, individual pages of document are locked in one microform and a duplicate can be easily created to keep in a secured location, microforms reduce the risk of mutilation and loss and increase the security of information (Smith, 1978).

7.3.8 *Other Applications of Microforms*

(i) Till recent days microforms used to help library cataloguing at multiple points and easy updating of catalogues, thus avoiding lengthy catalogue cabinets which, at times, do not allow for simultaneous consultation by more than a limited number of individuals.

(ii) Microforms are easy to store, handle and retrieve.

(iii) Microfilm technology itself used to be adopted for charging systems in libraries.

(iv) Microforms have ecological value and help to control paper pollution and paper cost. It also promotes recycling of paper by converting paper copies into microforms (Smith, 1978).

So far, the positive roles played by microforms from the angle of libraries are seen. No library can escape acquiring microform for providing effective and efficient information services for some more time.

7.4 Constraints of Microforms

Having seen the advantages of microforms, it is necessary to take note of the difficulties and threats posed by microforms:

(i) The biggest hurdle in adopting and promoting microforms is user resistance. It is more of psychology than physical inconvenience. Proper planning of 'micrographics system', conducive user-aid facility, environment and user orientation can reduce such resistance.

(ii) Non-availability of indigenous user equipment, inspection, cleaning, storing and other maintenance equipment required for handling microforms.

(iii) Libraries have very little control over quality, formats, types and reduction ratio of microforms when they are bought from outside agencies.

(iv) Standardisation and compatibility problems are also posed when microforms are procured from different sources.

(v) Libraries have to incur additional expenditure in maintaining environmental conditions such as temperature and humidity to safely store the microforms.

(vi) Microforms are inevitably damaged during reproduction and at times during usage. It is more so if the original negative is very old.

(vii) Fire risk continues to exist and in fact microforms are more susceptible to fire than hard copies.

(viii) The microforms technology is dynamic and it becomes difficult for smaller libraries to change their system, especially supporting user equipment facility with fast changing technology. In addition, there is a danger of over-sophistication. On the other hand, microforms themselves are likely to be outmoded by other newer media like optical/laser disc.

7.5 Sources for Selection of Microforms

There are plenty of sources for procuring microforms. In U.S.A. alone there are more than 100 micro-publishers. Most of them provide informative catalogues. In addition, several agencies publish microform selection tools. There are more than two million R&D reports, most of the theses and dissertations from U.S.A. and U.K., conference papers of professional organisations such as AIAA, IEEE, SAE, etc. over 12,000 periodical titles, 30,000 books and monographs, most of the standards and patents are available in microforms. A selected list of sources is given below:

(i) Guide to microforms in print and Subject guide to microforms in print, (The Microcard Corporation's cumulative annual listing of microforms)
(ii) National Register of Microform Masters (Library of Congress)
(iii) Micropublishers Trade List Annual (Microform Review)
(iv) Microform Market Place (Meckler Publishing Crop.)
(v) Serials in Microforms (UMI, covers over 12,000 titles)
(vi) Newspapers in Microform (LC)
(vii) Dissertation Abstracts International (UMI)
(viii) Secondary periodicals such as STAR, GRA&I, etc., which cover R&D reports
(ix) Individual micropublishers' catalogues, e.g., PP (Microforms Annual), AP, AIP, IEEE, ACS, IEE, Interscience, Elsevier, Springer Verlag, etc.
(x) Announcements in Micrographics journals, e.g.: IMC Journal; Journal of Micrographics (NMA); Microdoc (MAGB); Microform Patents; Microform Review; Micrographics Today (NMA); Information Media and Technology (Imtech); Serials Review.

(xi) Suzanne Dodson's Microforms Research Collections : A Guide

This presentation has not covered all aspects of micrographics system. Areas such as microfilm technology, organisation, maintenance, quality control and inspection of microforms, relation of micrographics with other systems of the library, preventive measures regarding the work hazards in micrographics, design of furniture for micrographics, layout for micrographics unit, copyright problems relating to micrographics, etc., are not covered.

It may be desirable here to say a few words about the situation in India. There is hardly any publisher in India who brings out publications in microform. However, there are agencies and organisations which can produce microforms from hard copies. Most of them cover only traditional formats such as films, jackets and rarely fiches. At present. special libraries are acquiring microforms mostly from suppliers abroad. Very few libraries are going for converting existing collection to microform. In the areas of user equipments, except few readers, nothing else, not even good quality storing and maintenance equipments are locally available. One is yet to see good quality indigenous equipment to promote use of microforms.

7.6 Development of Micrographics Facilities

Microforms have become almost inevitable for libraries. Most of the special libraries in India have either faced or are likely to face shortly the situation wherein part of their collection will be in microform. Whatever the justification a librarian putforths, the fact that microforms have been thrusted in the format, in the way and in the areas convenient to producers of information products of information rich countries greatly aided by Indian agents remains undisputed. Independent of whether users have welcomed microforms or not, they have entered most of the libraries mainly due to aggressive selling techniques of the trade. Of course, the advantages of microforms such as saving in space and economy have come handy for inevitable justification. In fact, more and more microforms are landing in libraries without much of planning for facilities to check them for quality, to store them safely and to promote their use.

The confrontation and frustration for a librarian, begins right from the time of their arrival in library as users either ignore them or resist using them in the same form and often demand paper copies, Unlike motion picture and TV where media attraction alone could sustain the interest of users in their initial years, microforms have least of medium attraction for users. Users are psychologically averse to microforms.

One of the reasons for user resistance, as mentioned repeatedly by experts, is lack of appropriate user aid equipment to read microforms and to take paper copies as and when needed. There is a total lack of indigenous technology and expertise to manufacture, instal, maintain and service quality user equipment facility, be it an acid free and fire resisting storing unit,' micrographics writing/marking pen, a handheld viewer, a cleaning aid, a reader, a microform projector, a reader-printer, an enlarger printer or an automated microform storing-cum-retrieval system. To cite a trivial problem is the need for micrographics pens to write accession number and/or possession mark of the library on microfiche. For long time, due to lack of a suitable indigenous aid, libraries use to either scratch fiche or stick pregummed labels damaging microfiche, or leave without accession number and/or possession mark.

Every librarian has to make independent efforts to discover the mystery of microform promotion and use as there is least of consolidation of experiences within the country. Non-availability of right information and right agency for a small library to make a quick and cost-efficient decision in setting up micrographics facilities is obvious. As a result, no quality check is made on microforms acquired and they are stored like index cards in many libraries. In some places microform collections are not even homogeneous as microforms of deferent format, polarity, reduction ratio are acquired. As regards buying user aids are concerned, whatever promoted by India agents are bought without much weightage for a critical evaluation. In this section, the discussion and illustrations are restricted to popular user aids such as microform readers and reader printers.

7.6.1 *Generation of Specifications*

Having acquired microforms and decided to promote their use with suitable user aid equipment, one has to generate the specifications of the equipment. Information about microform equipment is widely dispersed and a small or medium-sized library without a full-fledged micrographics unit and full time person to look after it, finds it very difficult to collect necessary information to decide on various aspects of microforms and generate necessary specifications for user equipment. In the absence of ready-made specifications and evaluated information about available equipment, established libraries within the country, micrographics associations, manufacturers and suppliers of micrographics equipment and journals in the field are some of the sources one can immediately look upon. A selected list of sources and a list of manufacturers and suppliers of micrographics equipment given as Appendixes would help to acquire product catalogues and other information. Even before one learns something about buying the best, if he has not planned well, agents might take the buyer for a ride. Unfortunately many libraries who had bad experience with a particular agent either keep silent or are even excessively generous to provide a good performance report making their way easy for further rides.

It is at this stage that the librarian should be clear about the nature of his existing as well as future microform collection in terms of formats, size, reduction ratio, polarity, film type, etc. A heterogeneous collection with many formats and types such as fiche, roll film, film cassette, aperture card with different reduction ratios will lead to maximum complexity in identifying multipurpose user aid equipment capable of satisfying all the requirements. The microform collection development policy has to be clear, consistent and definite to enable selection of user aid equipment. However, at times it becomes inevitable for a librarian to have more than one format or type of microform.

A check list of desirable features/specifications of microform reader and reader-printer is presented below. These features are not exhaustive nor a definite choice of feature is indicated. The nature of microform collection and needs of users should help individual libraries to modify features and decide additional features:

(i) *Film Format.* Though multipurpose readers such as those which allow fiche, aperture card and roll film, are available with necessary attachments, it is better to be specific about the main format to be handled by the reader.

(ii) *Screen.* (a) *Size:* For an approximate A4 size original to be blown up to one and a quarter time, a 11″ X 14″ screen is necessary. (b) *Type and Colour:* Front project type, nonglare, opaque or tinted light green or grey colour is preferable. Evaluate the advantages and disadvantages of rear projection type reader with front projection type reader and opaque screen with fresnel and diffusion type screens. (c) *Position and Angle:* Middle of the screen should not be above the eye level of user and the angle should be about 30 degrees backward for an opaque screen.

(iii) *Lens*. (a) *Magnification Ratio:* Depending on the reduction ratio of the microform appropriate magnification ratio of lens turret is preferable compared to floating and dropping type additional lenses. (b) *Resolution:* Resolution of lens should not be less than 4 lines per mm.

(iv) *Lamp*. (a) Tungsten halogen lamp with 50 watt power consumption should suffice an ordinary reader. (b) *Power Requirements:* 240/250 v, 50/60 HZ, AC. Chargeable battery operated models are also available especially for portable readers. (c) *Illumination:* Even illumination with control for high, low and off needed. (d) *Cooling Arrangement:* Internal/built-in-cooling arrangement by autofan is needed to keep the equipment cool while using continuously.

(v) *Ease of Handling*. (a) Easy insertion and safe handling of microform should be possible. (b) *Image Scan and Index Meter:* To access a particular frame (i.e., page) manual as well as motorised scanning facility with indexes are available. Motorised scan would be very useful in case of roll films. (c) *Image Rotation:* Provision to rotate image at least by 90 degrees is needed. This becomes critical when charts and tables have to be read. (d) We should be able to use microform reader with ambient light (i.e., without dark room) and without air conditioned atmosphere. (e) *Group Viewing:* In case group viewing facility is desired either an independent projector or a reader with limited projection facility can be considered.

(vi) *Physical features*. (a) *Dimension and Weight:* Physical features such as dimension and weight much depend on the purpose of readers. Accordingly, a range of readers such as pocket models, handheld viewers, portable brief case model readers and table model readers are available. (b) A dust cover and tool kit are normally provided with readers. (c) Spare lenses, lamps and necessary accessories such as roll film attachment mentioned earlier have to be asked for.

(vii) *Other Aspects*. (a) *Year of Introducing the Model:* It is always better to know the year of introducing the model and latest and long standing models are preferred in terms of availability of spares at a later date. (b) *Other Users:* Names and addresses of other users of the model in the vicinity within the country have to be obtained from suppliers for witnessing the working of the equipment and seeking performance reports. (c) *Indian Agent:* If there is any Indian agent the same has to be ascertained with agents commission, installation, order handling, training, annual service and other charges and ready availability of spares and consumables with Indian agent against Rupee payment. (d) Though looks as a formal purchase procedure, warranty and guarantee have to be asked from supplier. (e) One of the important aspects is to insist for complete specifications with printed catalogue of the equipment before making comparative evaluation. (f) It is also better to insist for arranging a demonstration, if possible.

Further, in case of reader-printer the following additional features/specifications have to be added:

(i) *Exposure Control:* Provision for controlling exposure while printing paper copy is desirable.

(ii) *Print Delivery Speed or Print Cycle Time:* Some reader-printers could be quite slow allowing one to take 150-200 copies per day. Many do not allow image to be read while printing and the same contributes to slow print delivery.

(iii) *Copy Counter:* A built-in counter to account for number of copies taken is desirable.

(iv) *Copying Process:* Different processes such as wet and dry silver process, electrolytic or electrochemical process, electrostatic or xerographic process and diazo process have their own advantages and disadvantages.

(v) *Cost Per Copy.* Normally supplier's/agent's estimation of cost per copy is an underestimation.

(vi) *Consumables:* Type of paper, maximum and minimum size of paper allowed, shelf life and supply period of coated paper, if any, and other consumables have to be seen. If all the consumables are indigenously available or available on Rupee payment at reasonable price it goes to the advanta f buying library.

(vii) *Other Features:* The copy quality especially legibility, durability and polarity on copying much depends on the copying process. Does the reader-printer allow copying from both positive as well as negative microform is another important consideration.

7.6.2 *Evaluation of Offers*

After obtaining offers from as many vendors of micrographic equipment as possible as per the existing purchase procedure of the parent organisation, the offers have to be critically evaluated against indenting specifications and needs of the micrographics facility. The first hurdle in this process is fictious offers and counter or alternate offers. Fictitious offers are of the type where an Indian agent without finalising his agency would submit quotation and an indigenous offer might also come just to stop you from importing. We had once experienced still a third variety, wherein we had selected an item to import through an Indian agent and went through the ordeal process of obtaining DGTD clearance, FE release and a valid user licence by spending more than an year. Unfortunately, after collecting order, licence and all other necessary documents, the agent regretted that they no more represented the principal (or lost the agency!). The counter offers are those where, if you ask for a microfiche projector, one would quote for a brief case model microfiche reader explaining how it can also be used as a projector for group viewing and if you ask for an automated microfiche storing, retrieving and displaying unit (with enlarger-printer function), the supplier would quote for a passive card cabinet for storing and a separate enlarger-printer. At times, counter offers can create enough confusion to conclude that indenting specifications are wrong. Thus eliminating all fictious and counter offers and offers not meeting the requirements, one should proceed to evaluate remaining offers.

It is always safe to insist for full specifications and a printed catalogue for all the equipment before evaluation. Once a comparative assessment is ready, parties should be requested for arranging a demonstration and/or the same models in use at other places may be examined. Obtaining performance reports from other users of the equipment is quite useful provided, as mentioned earlier, you expect a very frank opinion. Quite often other users might give either vague or favourable reports to avoid displeasing the suppliers.

At this stage, critical evaluations appearing in professional journals and those obtained from professional bodies mentioned in Appendix would be quite useful. Once we had obtained expert opinion of one of internationally reputed professional bodies while buying an item. Surprisingly, the equipment later failed miserably for about 3 years not only with us but also with other two buyers in the country. The agent when failed to successfully instal and test the machine came up with so many reasons including the fact that the model is a refurbished one and no more manufactured by his principal. It may be noted here that what has been found good in UK or USA may fail to perform well in India for many reasons including the fact that manufacturing and shipping places might be different for us. For example, all units to India are shipped from Singapore factory of some multinational companies.

Finally, while evaluating offers, compromises of minor requirements and trade off with price become inevitable. One has to make judicious choice keeping all the data mentioned above in view.

7.6.3 *Indigenous or Imported?*

At this juncture, it is worth digressing and discussing whether to go for indigenous micrographics equipment or imported ones and, if imported, whether to restrict to import through agents or to explore the possibility of importing directly where there are no Indian agents. Till date, indigenous micrographics equipment and their consumables of acceptable quality are not available. Even simple storing equipment which are heat resistant, fire proof and acid free and cleaning and writing aids are not available. The growth of indigenous manufacturers of micrographics equipment is very slow compared to that in the reprographics area.

Once convinced about need for an imported equipment, naturally one would play safe to go through Indian agents. As against this, it is always highly economical and worth exploring wider market for direct import of such items which do not need extensive installation, training and post-sale servicing. Thus all consumable items, simple handheld viewers, cleaning aids, micrographics pens, portable/brief case model readers and even table model readers can be imported directly at a much cheaper price than going through Indian agents. In one case, price (excluding duty) of a microfiche reader quoted by an Indian agent (not exclusive) was almost three times higher than that quoted by the manufacturer abroad. However, items like reader-printer need an agent for installing, training the operator and for want of post sale service.

7.6.4 *Importing Formalities*

If decided to import directly or through an agent, then a series of procedural import formalities have to be met. Many a times, decision to import directly is adversely affected by aversion to lengthy or ordeal import procedures. The process starts with justifying the need with one's own authorities. Then the need for importing the same has to be convinced at the parent organisation level. At this stage, it is better to have clarity on the import provision with the help of up to date import manual and policy handbook of Government of India. In any case, items totally banned should be checked and eliminated. Even items under restricted list need a detailed and lengthy justification. However, all such items which are listed under OGL could be processed without much difficulty. Quite often, import restrictions are not enumerative but only indicative and hence at different stages the same can be interpreted to have been covered under different lists of import handbook.

It is always desirable to procure light-weight items, delicate items such as lenses which are likely to be damaged by humidity and rough handling and also those consumables which have short shelf life by air freight. Though minor, this aspect should not be overlooked.

Having justified the item with authorities, depending on the procedure of the parent organisation, FE for the required CIF value of the item has to be obtained. If the item is not under OGL, then application for user licence has to be filed. A very detailed write up with justification for importing such an item, the consequences of not importing, description of item and catalogue of the item have to be submitted to DGTD for obtaining a NMI certificate, and CDE certificate, if customs duty exemption is applicable to buyer. DGTD might turn down the request for NMI certificate citing names of Indian manufacturers for the item. If the potential buyer is sure that the products of these Indian firms are not suitable or they are yet to be marketed, the fact has to be effectively established by obtaining the actual offers of Indian manufacturers and places of existing installations. Some of these firms might have obtained licence, or applied for licence or a letter of intent might have been submitted to manufacture the said items. In one of the cases, we approached the Indian manufacturers indicated by DGTD and found no response over long time. However, if there is a comparable product within the country, the same need to be acquired dropping the idea of importing.

At this stage, it is necessary for R&D organisations, educational institutions and their libraries to note the special provisions of import for them against OGL and user licence and accordingly apply for import licence as well as customs duty exemption. Yet an amount approximately equal to duty expected should be kept aside in the budget. Often customs duty paid at the time of clearance can be got refunded later depending on type of equipment and nature of buying organisation. Even at the time of customs clearance, there could be uncertainties about the rate of duty applicable. An interaction with customs authorities with an explanation about nature of item would help to minimise the duty as per provision.

7.6.5 *Maintenance and Post-sale Service*

As mentioned earlier, some equipment have to be bought through Indian agents either to avail their installation, maintenance and post-sale service or as a consequence of exclusive agency or both. It is appropriate to discuss some of the problems connected with maintenance and servicing by Indian agents.

At the outset, one need not be surprised if a service engineer of an Indian agent starts experimenting by trial and error method with one's equipment in case it is one of the first few to have arrived in the country. Normally, not all the service engineers are trained abroad by the manufacturers. Apart from senior service engineer learning and training their new batches of service engineers the agent could use the buyer's facility as sales promoting demonstration unit for other potential buyers. At times this becomes a nuisance. Interestingly, the turnover of service and sales personnel is so high that one wonders whether agents act like training schools with customer facilities as laboratories.

Though one acquires all the recommended strategic spares, many a times the equipment will be down for want of a different spare or a spare exhausted. Not only a library has to spend on many unutilised spares but also has to wait for about 3 to 6 months till necessary spares are acquired, if the same is not stocked by Indian agent. A capital equipment may lay idle for want of a pair of small toothed gear made of plastic or tuflon. Very rarely, agents stock spares for the equipment they are suppose to represent and service.

Many Indian agencies are immaturely changed or cancelled. As cited earlier, in one of the cases, the agency is forfeited (or lost) by the agent even before the first unit arrived in the country. The result is that we have to forego, all our efforts in obtaining an user licence. (Some agents listed in Appendix might have already changed!).

Another problem is that once we are wedded to a particular make of equipment, the cost of consumables, spares and even annual service contract can be hiked considerably at random. Once we had an offer from an Indian agent for a reader printer with unusual 30 per cent commission on landed cost. Though party has originally claimed that it is DGS&D approved rate, later declined to produce proof. Hence we were forced go back to retendering the item. For all the reasons discussed above, the overall post-sale service of many Indian agents is found grossly inadequate and unsatisfactory.

8

VENDOR CONTROLLED ORDER PLANS

8.1 Need for Vendor Controlled Order Plans

Increased prices, inelastic budgets and inflation are increasingly constraining the buying powers of libraries. Naturally, libraries have to explore more and more gratis and exchange modes of acquisition, especially for unconventional gray literature. When inevitable, reading materials are bought directly or through vendors/agents either on credit basis or on advance payment basis. Some conservative suppliers/agencies have deposit account schemes and prepaid coupon systems. Irrespective of the size of a library, more desirable and possibly least exploited methods of procurement, which can considerably enhance the utility of limited monetary resources, are standing/blanket orders, package deals, combination subscriptions, membership orders and other vendor controlled order plans.

Normally, specialists confine to selection of books in their respective areas of specialisation, which are quite narrow, rather than interested in the overall collection development of libraries. Collection development, in the strict sense, involves costly, time consuming and specialist labour intensive judicial selection activity. Reviewing and evaluating all the books published in any area is very difficult. Thus, delegating initial identification of current reading materials to vendors frees library staff and specialists from the arduous task so that they can carry out actual selection of current, retrospective, specific and serial titles more efficiently (Cargel, 1979). Of course, the delegation is meaningful if the vendors are well organised and are competent to do the task. The dealer library (approval) plan is supposed to help in achieving this objective and it is basically a blanket or standing order arrangement. A standing order is normally placed for a series while a blanket order is placed in terms of a subject field, grade level, country's publications or publisher's publications. Standing orders "... operate on the principle that all publications in a series represent similar quality and potential interest to the collection – that is, if it is worth having one volume, it is usually worth having the whole series" (McClung, 1985, p. 10).

8.2 Advantages and Disadvantages of Blanket and other Vendor Controlled Order Plans

The main advantages of blanket orders are: (i) Automatic receipt of relevant documents and no chance of missing a relevant book published. (ii) Saving in office work with fewer invoices and no separate orders. (iii) Saving in price. (iv) Saving in time of staff from selection work. (v) Cutting delays in supply of books. (vi) Eliminating pre-order searching. (vii) Helps developing a profile of library and reviewing collection development policy of library.

The main disadvantages of blanket orders are: (I) Uncertainties regarding number, cost and relevance of books. (ii) Library may have to accommodate irrelevant and/or duplicate items supplied under blanket order and yet, a relevant title may not be supplied. (ii) Blanket order may create a budgetary problem with abnormal increase in price and number of books supplied. (iii) At times, it may cost more in terms of service charges and accommodating irrelevant items supplied than that saved. (iv) A library may incur more cost in terms of time and efforts needed to process and organise irrelevant items than that saved. (v) Precious storing space of library would be consumed by irrelevant items supplied against blanket orders. (vi) Scope or slant of a series may change and such unpredictability and unreliability may cause unexpected gaps in collection. (vii) Integrating such plans with individual orders and deciding how long to wait for an important item/title under such plans are difficult.

Thus a discretionary, intelligent and judicial judgment on blanket/standing and other vendor controlled order plans is necessary.

8.3 Different Types of Vendor Controlled Order Plans

It is a common practice in many libraries to place standing orders for advances, annual reviews and other serial titles, including directories and handbooks, to avoid routine ordering work and to make marginal savings. However, certain package deal offers, such as those offered by professional bodies (e.g. IEEE and AIAA) and membership offers (individual, student, associate, institutional, patron membership of ACM, BSI, etc.), provide considerable saving in price, procurement time and office work. Combination subscriptions, such as those for SIAM journals, also result in considerable saving.

Much less known terms in Indian libraries are 'Greenaway plan' 'Till Forbidden' order and 'Gathering plan'. The greenaway plan is a contract between a library and a publisher for a library to buy, at a large discount, one copy of all or most of the publisher's trade books. The purpose is to provide examination copies immediately after publication so that the library can decide which titles should be acquired in multiple copies. If the library does not buy multiple copies, however, publishers will cancel the agreement. 'Till Forbidden' is used by a library in serials work to indicate that the publisher or supplier of a journal should automatically renew a subscription without any further approval from the library (Evans, 1987, p. 109). 'Gathering plan' means a blanket order arrangement with a foreign dealer, who is, in effect, given instructions to gather and ship whatever can be obtained in specified categories. All the above plans are vendor controlled order plans. Another vendor originated book supply plan not practiced in India is the lease or rental plan designed to provide regularly changing collections of best sellers.

8.4 Dealer Library Plan

It may be desirable to discuss certain issues relating to popular 'dealer library plan' or 'approval plan' in the Indian context. Most of the vendors use 'approval plan' as a tool for promoting sale of leftover items with them. Vendors are quite poor in building up profiles of libraries for 'approval plans'. They neither have dealer's thesaurus to enable libraries to select subject descriptors nor allow for any non-subject modifiers like academic level, publisher, country of origin, language of publication, geographic and time limitations, subject treatment, physical format, price, etc., in building profiles of libraries. Though approval plans should exclude unrevised new editions, reprints, government publications, dissertations, translations, serials, textbooks, juvenile and popular books, many vendors do not strictly adhere to such understanding as well as to profiles. As a result the predictability and dependability of approval plans are poor. Further a good approval plan should result in less than 10 per cent rejections. But in practice more than 50 per cent (at times even up to 80% or 90%) of items received on approval basis get rejected wasting precious space and labour of libraries. For lack of proper assessment of approval plans libraries are not able to restrict approval plans to two or three vendors.

8.5 Evaluation of Vendor Controlled Order Plans

In choosing a vendor for approval plan an informal evaluation of vendors has to be done by the library based on their bibliographic accuracy, speed of delivery, return rates, various operating procedures, profiling techniques/capabilities and quick arrangement for notification of new items. Approval plans can also be assessed by comparing approval plan receipts with staff members' perceptions of what should have been received. Another formal way of assessing approval plans is to compare library circulation data of approval plan materials with items specifically requested by users. One study has reported that the books that arrived through approval plan were the least likely new acquisitions to circulate (Evans, 1970). In another study it was found that approval plans tend to be least satisfactory in science subjects (Evans and Argyres, 1974).

Thus it is not difficult for a library to evaluate vendor controlled order plans such as dealer library plan, package/bulk/standing/membership/combination and other orders. Membership and such similar offers are normally available from not-for-profit organisations and publishers and some times only to not-for-profit organisations or individuals. Apart from monetary considerations of reduced price, the offers extend free postage, handling and quick supply on credit basis. At times, additional copies are made available free or at reduced rate and some documents are available only to members or package deal customers, that too in special 'library edition'. Some of them also extend referral service to members. A continuous or periodic evaluation of all such blanket/standing orders, memberships, etc. through a cost-benefit study is necessary in special libraries so as to make sure that the disadvantages of such blanket orders do not overtake or offset the advantages.

8.6 A Case Study of Standing Order Procurement of NASA Reports

NTIS, the largest gray literature handling agency, offers a series of standing orders which include JPRS, FBIS, CIA monographs, NASA-FS and SRIM (which has the additional advantage of saving due to supply in microform). The economies in procurement of technical reports in general and SRIM in particular have already been dealt in Chapter 6. Apart from contacting the appropriate source, opting for a suitable standing order enhances the system efficiency. However, changed conditions have to be noted and a trial order needs to be placed. NTIS does not entertain direct enquiries from Indian libraries and often agents are not much up to date and informed.

NASA reports are naturally the life blood for a space science and satellite technology library. The relative importance of NASA reports is evident from the results of a use study of paper copy reports of ISAC library based on a 20 per cent systematic random sample (Sridhar, 1981). Though the overall usage of reports is less, NASA reports, which formed about 27 per cent of sample, were used to the extent of 55 per cent of total use of the entire sample. In other words, NASA reports were the maximum sought after reports in the library. As such, NASA FS standing order service has been availed of by the library since 1981. As NTIS has doubled the price of the service since 1983, it became necessary to evaluate this trial standing order service.

8.6.1 *NASA Information System*

It may not be out of context to mention here a few words about the NASA information facility itself (NASA, STIO, nd). The STIO of NASA collects nearly one lakh documents per year from government organisations, universities, research laboratories, corporations and commercial publishers in U.S.A. and from more than 200 foreign countries. The actual task of acquiring and processing is done by STIF, a contractor-operated NASA installation, TIS of AIAA and ESA, which have exchange agreements with STIO.

NASA keeps most of its collection in microform and bibliographic data in machinable form. It does not supply its documents directly to users abroad. One has to buy them through NTIS or SOD (USGPO). The results of NASA sponsored research are recorded in approximately 10,000 technical reports each year.

These reports are obtainable through NTIS (Kent and Lancour, 1980, p. 168). As learnt from one of the Indian agents of NTIS, 3500-4500 NASA reports are input into the NTIS system per year. Thus, NTIS lacks more than 50 per cent of current NASA reports.

STAR, a semi-monthly announcement bulletin of NASA, covers about 25,000 citations to unclassified reports, patents, translations and standards per year. *LSTAR* is a quarterly bulletin of NASA for unclassified but limited distribution and security classified reports acquired by STIF. It covers citations of less than a thousand to a few thousand reports a year, which are normally not re-announced in STAR when restrictions are removed. About 90 per cent of reports announced in LSTAR originate from DOD and the remaining are NASA in-house and contractor reports.

All the reports listed in *STAR* are not available to public. *STAR* uses # symbol to indicate that a document is available only in microfiche, * to indicate that the report has originated within NASA or one of its prime contractors and + to indicate unusual problems of reproducibility and the documents being available only in paper copies.

8.6.2 *NASA-FS Standing Order Service*

The main feature of NASA-FS service of NTIS is that selected unclassified (probably more popular) reports of NASA sponsored research in some selected series in original printed form are regularly (once in a month) mailed from NASA to the customer through NTIS at a flat rate per report irrespective of its size. NASA-FS service includes supply of reports in popular NASA series, such as CP, CR, RP, SP, TM, TP, and few others. Though it is claimed that the service covers reports in TN and TT series also, they were not received at ISAC Library.

It is worth taking note of the nature of different series of NASA reports covered in the service. CPs are compilations of scientific and technical papers or transcripts arising from conferences, workshops, symposia, seminars and other professional meetings that NASA elects to publish. CRs contain results of work completed under NASA contracts or grants. The service covers CRs numbered below 50,000 which are printed and considered substantively important. RPs include technical handbooks and manuals, critical tables, monographs and scientific and technical textbooks. SPs include scientific summaries of mission results, scientific photography, atlases and histories and chronologies. In particular, new information resulting from space exploration and significant advances in space science and technology (below 3,000 numbers), handbooks, charts and data compilations on various aspects of science and technology (numbered 3,000s), histories and chronologies (numbered 4,000s), management and evaluation standards providing significant advances for decision-makers in system and program management, design, development, manufacture and evaluation (numbered 6,000s) and such of the SP reports printed by SOD (USGPO) are also covered under SP series. TMs are in-house reports with classified, preliminary or unconfirmed research results and the service obviously covers such reports which are unclassified and unlimited (numbered above 50,000). The technical publications under TP and a few other series are also included in the service. TNs present high quality completed technical results but less broad in scope than TRs and TTs, (numbered below 8,000, which provide English translations of foreign documents with broad significance for NASA's programs) are also supposed to have been covered in this service. One important point to be noted here is that all the reports brought out in these series as per the scope mentioned are not supplied under NASA-FS service and the criteria for inclusion or exclusion of a report are not clear. Of late, NASA-FS standing order is allowed to be restricted to broad subjects specified by NTIS.

In other words, the following series are specifically excluded from NASA-FS service. (i) CRs above 50,000 which contain preliminary, unconfirmed or proprietary information and hence have limits on their distribution, (ii) SPs which fall under technology utilization series (numbered 5,000s) and spacecraft design criteria in four areas of technology – environment, structures, guidance and control and chemical propulsion (numbered 8,000s), (iii) TMs below 50,000 which are not printed but are available only in microfiche and duplicated form, (iv) TRs which are unclassified final reports that provide comprehensive coverage of NASA research project or other information of current and lasting importance to aeronautics or space science, (v) TTs which may have narrower interest and distribution limitations (numbered 8,000s) and are not printed, but are available in microfiche or duplicated form, and (vi) NASA patents.

The foregoing discussion of the scope of NASA-FS service gives an idea of the types of NASA reports expected in the standing order service. A look at the quantum of reports and the financial implications of NASA-FS service is worth. This standing order has brought 425 reports in 1981 and 247 in 1982 at $10 per report. The number of reports during 1983, 1984 and 1985 were 382, 357 and 312 respectively at $20 per report. This service has under-gone several changes during the last few years and as a result the total number of reports is believed to have come down considerably. NTIS, as a commercial organisation, might be discouraging this service, as is evident from the fact that the flat rate of $10 per report in 1982 has been doubled ($20) in 1983 and the same has prompted this analysis and evaluation. The price is further revised to $23 in 1986 and $30 in 1989.

On the other hand, SRIM service, which is also a standing order service, is for microfiche copies of reports falling under specified subject groups or those originating from a specified organisation (e.g., NASA) supplied at a flat rate of $1.80 in 1982, $2 in 1983, $2.20 in 1984 and 1985, $2.50 in 1986 and $2.60 in 1989 per report. But reports supplied in SRIM service are not necessarily current reports. There is a considerable time lag in the supply of NASA reports under SRIM service compared to that supplied under NASA-FS service. About 4,000 NASA reports per year are expected under SRIM if all NASA reports are specified. Most of the reports available under NASA-FS service are not made available in SRIM service. For example, in the month of May 1982, only one report became common between NASA-FS service and SRIM service for NASA reports.

8.6.3 *Economic Aspects of the Decision*

In order to facilitate taking the decision regarding whether or not to continue subscription to NASA-FS at increased price, the actual reports supplied for about six months during 1983 in different series were examined. The assessment has shown that about 59 per cent of reports were fairly relevant to ISAC library and the library would have otherwise also acquired in case announcement bulletins were regularly scanned. The breakup of this relevance among different series, is presented in Table 8.1, which also incorporates the percentage of supply in different series and average size/price (with code) for different series for buying the reports individually. Hence, this model has been based on estimated percentage of relevant reports and estimated average price for each series.

TABLE 8.1: Decision Model 1: Probable Cost of Relevant NASA Reports Based on Probability of Occurrence of a Series and its Average Cost

Series	Supplies in 1983		% of relevant reports	Average size/price		Cost of relevant reports in $, i.e. (2)X(4)X(6) / 100
	No.	%		Code	1983 price in $	
1	2	3	4	5	6	7
CP	36	9.4	80	A18	62	1786
CR	93	24.3	52	A09	35	1693
RP	17	4.4	83	A06	26	367
SP	10	2.6	83	A09	35	291
TM	79	20.7	62	A07	29	1420
TP	146	38.2	46	A05	23	1545
Others	1	0.3	100	A04	20	20
Total	382	99.9	57	—	—	7122

It is seen from Table 8.1, that it would have costed $7,122 to buy 218 relevant reports individually (out of 382 reports supplied under NASA-FS standing order). On the other hand, the standing order (for 1983) has costed $7,640 at the rate of $20 per report (for 382 reports). In both the cases, the mandatory air freight charges are excluded. Thus, there is a marginal loss of $518 ($7,640–7,122) towards the remaining 164 less relevant and irrelevant reports. Another dimension of the cost not indicated in this analysis is the cost of processing and storing irrelevant reports. However, if the procedure permits, the library can avoid this cost by not taking irrelevant reports to the stock but to give them away to other libraries for which they are potentially useful, either as gift or at a reduced price, and recover a substantial part of the expenditure on NASA-FS service. Hence, as per Decision Model 1, it is still not clearly beneficial to ISAC library to continue with NASA-FS service unless the cost of less relevant and irrelevant reports is recovered. It is but natural that the savings and advantages of the service would have been enormous had the service continued at the 1982 price of $10 or even at a marginal increase in price per report instead of $20. While the price of a report for individual purchase has been marginally increased by $2 per report, irrespective of size, the price per report in NASA-FS service has been increased by $10 per report in 1983.

An alternative decision model is presented in Table 8.2, which is based on probability of price group of reports supplied if the same have to be bought individually. This model emphasizes the price distribution of reports supplied and not the distribution of percentage of relevance among reports of different series.

If ISAC library has to buy all 1983 NASA reports obtained through NASA-FS service on individual price basis, as per Table 8.2, it would have costed \$9,788. Hence there is a saving of \$2,148 (i.e., \$9,788 – 7,640), provided all the 382 reports were relevant and useful. Since only 59 per cent (i.e., 218) of them were found relevant and useful, the proportional cost has to be worked out and examined.

Table 8.2 shows \$50 as the median cost of a report and based on this the total cost of 218 relevant reports would have been \$10,900, which shows a saving of \$3,260 (i.e., \$10,900 – 7,640). Another version of Model 2 can also be worked out based on the mode cost of \$17 per report. According to this, the relevant reports would cost only \$3,706, showing a loss of \$3,934 (i.e., \$7,640 – 3,706) towards less relevant and irrelevant reports.

Table 8.2 also reveals the weighted average price of a report as \$25.5. It is shown in an earlier Chapter on technical reports that the average report from NTIS through Indian agents costed about \$23 (excluding mandatory air freight charges). Thus, it establishes, incidentally, a fact which otherwise would have led to suspicion that the supplier might push less costly reports in a standing order deal like NASA-FS service.

The third version of the model based on the (weighted average/mean) shows that \$5,559 would have been sufficient to buy all relevant reports. This leads to a loss of \$2,081 (i.e., \$7,640 – 5,559) due to 164 less relevant and irrelevant reports. The third version of the model based on mean is statistically more dependable than versions 1 and 2.

A consolidation of the results of both the models is presented in Table 8.3 ignoring version 2 and 3 of Model 2. Since Model 1 is based on probability of a series and the average cost of a report in a given series, whereas Model 2 is based on probability of individual purchase cost of a given report, the first model is aggressive and the second one is conservative.

By either model, the NASA-FS service is not cost efficient or economically justifiable and the library incurs a loss of \$518/2081 towards less relevant and irrelevant reports. One should note here that the errors in the estimates, including the estimate of relevant

printed reports are supplied against stray orders only rarely. Lastly, the one-sided loose copies of reports supplied by NTIS against individual orders invariably need immediate binding before they are released for use, involving additional delay and cost.

Before taking a final decision, the results and observations involving all the above economic and non-economic considerations were presented before a user-representative committee. The committee decided not to cancel the NASA-FS service. Many users have strongly felt that some of the reports under this service are invaluable sources of information. It has also been reviewed and assessed once again recently to confirm the strong need for such standing order procurement of NASA reports.

9

JOURNAL SUBSCRIPTION

Problems of journal subscription in special libraries, for various reasons, need a special mention. Specialised journals are the most important primary media of recording, communicating and archiving S&T information. Journal subscription consumes more than half of the reading material budget of a special library, poses high degree of risk due to advance payments, and results in supply of individual issues of journals over an year in a continuous way. They are costly in terms of price, handling and storage. Journals are differentiated and yet unique products of several publishers. Journal subscription is also very much in the seller's market and publishers dictate price and terms. The policies of publishers are so diverse that the libraries are required to suitably modify their own procedures and terms in dealing with diverse set of publishers. Specialised journals usually have limited markets consisting mostly of institutions and libraries. There is a steep, steady and phenomenal increase in prices of journals over years. There are frequent changes in publishers' appointment of agents – local, foreign, exclusive, preferred, etc. For many such reasons, the discussion of problems of collection development is incomplete without the discussion of problems of journal subscription. In addition to general problems discussed in an earlier chapter, some specific problems relating to journal subscription are presented here. The problems like transit loss, deciding whether to subscribe journals though agent or directly, etc., assume double importance in journal subscription due to invariable advance payments to be made. When supplies are made on credit basis like that of books, obtaining them through agents do not cause much risk on the part of libraries and any transit loss is understood to be borne by the supplier. That is not the case with journals.

9.1 To have an Agent or Not?

The first and foremost problem of journal subscription faced by libraries is to decide whether to have an agent (Indian or foreign) or to go directly with publishers. There are advantages in both ways, but some are more visible and others are not. Journal subscription is overburdened with the need for extensive communication and correspondence and any effort to reduce communication causes reduction in efficiency. The processing ('fixed') cost of serials is much more than that of monographs. Such correspondence does cost library in terms of manpower, material and postage. But one does not notice them as they are invisible costs. For the same reason ". . . for most libraries, it is not economical to place serial subscription directly with the publisher" (Evans, 1987, p. 169). Yet by subscribing through an agent libraries are not relieved of their responsibilities of keeping extensive serials records in an accurate and up to date manner (Magrill and Hickey, 1984, p. 167). There is a general conflict between cost orientation and service orientation in handling journal subscription. One major problem in choosing an agent is the risk of huge advance payments. There are enough cases of cheating libraries, in spite of taking precautions like obtaining bank guarantee and insisting on evidential proof of having transmitted payments to the publishers before collecting payment from library, etc. Some agents are believed to deliberately delay transmitting payments to publishers. Often agents have no more 'control'/knowledge/information over/about publishers than libraries and hence their role is increasingly limited to transfer of subscription amount from libraries to publishers and some information from publishers to libraries. Some agents limit their service to the placement, renewal and payment of subscriptions and prefer not to try to solve problems relating to missing issues or other subscription irregularities. However, the advantages of subscribing to journals through vendors include simple 'one order, one invoice and one check' for multiple subscriptions, automatic renewal with or without multiple year subscription rate, assistance in making claims and free information about discontinuations, mergers, changes in frequency and price, free subject-wise lists, etc. In addition, agents should be chosen not based on lowest bid but on the quick and prompt action taken to renew journals and place orders, speed with which claims are handled and other service considerations. "Agents with poor performance histories should be avoided whenever possible since it may cost the library a great deal of time, money and efforts to 'straighten out' its subscriptions once they are confused by an ineffective agent" (Magrill and Hickey, 1984, p. 168-169). How much service an agent can provide without additional charges and whether his system is automated to provide information quickly should also be seen.

On the other hand, the degree of risk of advance payments is not reduced with foreign agents and even publishers. Yet claims for non-supply or refund and other problems can be directly addressed to publishers where journals are directly subscribed with publishers. There are also fears that agents may not quickly, adequately and strongly represent non-supply and refund claims of libraries with publishers. Allowing agents to receive supply at their end for forwarding to libraries may block many useful free information mailed by publishers apart from further increasing the risk of advance payments, problems of checking the prices, adding to delay in supplies and totally cutting off libraries from publishers if subscription is not entered in their names. Further, some foreign agents not only markup prices but also levy substantial handling charges. Under these circumstances it is extremely difficult to give all time, efficient and effective way of subscribing to journals. Each library has to explore its options and evaluate available sources and agents making a tradeoff among cost (including invisible cost), quality of service, ability to take risk, budgetary and procedural constraints, etc.

9.2 Risk of Advance Payments and Delayed Transmission of Payments by Agents

As mentioned earlier, journals invariably require advance payments. Whether it is with publishers or with agents advance payments made without proper security runs considerable risk. Calculated risk has to be taken by every library based on past experience and informal assessment of health of agent or publisher.

There is also a general complaint that some agents collect subscription amount much in advance and pass on to publishers after a gap of three to six months so that the money can be profitably utilised in their business. Such delayed transmission of payments by agents does cause delayed supply or non-supply of initial issues of the year. To overcome this difficulty, the practice of obtaining bank guarantee and/or requesting the agent to first pay to the publisher on behalf of library and then collect the payment from libraries has been devised. Of late, here and there cases of cheating in the later method with bogus payment details have also come to light. In either case assessing the credibility and soundness of an agent or publisher in order to take calculated limited risk is necessary. On the other hand, many agents complain about delayed processing of renewal orders and payment by libraries causing delayed supply or non-supply of initial issues of the year. In other words, delayed payment is a problem which can also be caused at the end of libraries. Publishers usually require subscription payments six to eight weeks in advance of the commencement of subscription period or volume of the journal, so as to enable them to make better estimates of number of copies to be printed.

9.3 Delayed Supply, Non-supply, Transit Loss and Refunds

Having chosen to subscribe journals either directly with publishers, or through agents or a combination of both, a major problem is irregularity in supply and transit loss. As mentioned in an earlier Chapter, it is not economical to go for insured supplies of journals, as transit loss never exceed 5 per cent of supplies. Secondly large majority of publishers freely replace journal issues not received by libraries. But many foreign publishers expect such claims to reach them within 60 to 90 days of publishing an issue of a journal. At times, this is quite tricky and unreasonable. If a journal is irregular or behind schedule, a library may not be able to guess when a particular issue of journal is out of press. Even where a journal is regular and expected date of publication can be guessed, 60 to 90 days limit may be acceptable to libraries within the country of publisher or libraries of neighbouring countries and to libraries which subscribe to them by airmail. For example, for a sea mail subscription to an U.S.A. journal, an Indian library cannot send reminders or make non-supply claim within 60-90 days as sea mail itself takes 3-4 months to reach India from U.S.A. It is pains-taking, time consuming and perpetual activity to educate such publishers about liberal time limit needed for making claims of non-supply from far away countries. If a library is over cautious and sends reminders and claims well before 60 to 90 days it is either bound to receive a reply that issues are just mailed and requesting to wait for their receipt or to accumulate unwanted duplicate copies of journal issues. Above all, there are some publishers like the American Society for Non-destructive Testing Inc, who do not allow or permit their overseas subscribers or members to file claims for missing issues. Brown and Smith (1980) enumerate a number of problems and proposals in respect of making claims for missing issues.

Most of the publishers do not maintain extensive files and records regarding subscribers/customers as it costs them heavily. If a typical Indian library chooses to write letter referring various earlier correspondences, the letter will not be even understood by the publisher. Every letter needs to be complete and self contained in respect of issues raised and provide subscriber reference number and/or a copy of mailing label. Whether it is library or agent the claim should be worded in such a way that replacement copy or at least soiled copy be sent failing which extension of subscription or refund should be made. Often, errors take place at publishers end in recording subscription or renewal of journals including those of duplicate or overlapping subscriptions. It may be about address, period of subscription, number of copies, extension of subscription in view of non-supply, etc. It takes a long time and a number of letters to get the subscription record of publishers rectified. Normally publishers abroad do not care for clarifying the issues and sending replies to letters from Indian libraries for reasons explained above. Unsatisfactory response to claims and the resultant gaps in collection are too frustrating to special libraries in India.

Delayed supply of issues may occur due to delays in publishing journal itself. If libraries do not take enough care at the time of renewal to insist on clearing pending supplies, overpayment accumulates at publishers' end and occasionally publishers may close down or sell out their journals without properly passing on credits to the subscribers. If a journal is ceased or publication suspended before expiry of subscription, there is very little one can do about it. Rarely one may even face a situation in which all letters and reminders of libraries either being returned stating addressee moved or not found or no replies are received for such communication.

Where publishers care to reply to subscribing libraries, in majority of the cases, the standing reply is that issues have been mailed upon publication. Some of them would give the date of mailing and few even produce proof for having mailed. Most of them complain on Indian postal authorities for non-supply or loss and request libraries to check at local post office. Occasionally, publishers do initiate an enquiry with postal authorities in their country which normally lands up in production of proof for having mailed/sent to their counterparts in the country.

Often, damages to mailing label and wrappers during transit of journals (mostly in surface mail) take place due to poor packing by some publishers leading to huge accumulation of such unidentifiable parcels in dead letter dock. Wrong delivery within the country and even within the organisation by local mail distributing agency are not unusual. Some even suspect deliberate lifting of journals from mail in case of popular magazines like *National Geographic*. A detailed account of different types of mails, problems relating to mail sorting and distribution as applied to transit loss of journals can be seen in Brown and Smith (1980).

Transit loss of journals create a vicious circle in deciding the responsibility for loss. As they are not insured, publishers (though in most of the cases they are generous to send replacement copies or provide extension of subscription) can washoff their hands. If the subscription is through agents and if there is no clear agreement on who should bear transit loss, it is quite difficult to sort out. Obviously, agent prefer to get all the journals at their end and distribute them if they have to take the responsibility for transit loss. As explained earlier this option puts off library from the publishers record for all practical purposes. However, some preferential and exclusive agents, as a rule, get journal issues at their end for subsequent redistribution within the country. Even in such situations some abnormalities like making false claims for having distributed are noticed.

During renewal of journals, usually once in a year, another vicious circle will be created where supply for previous year/s is not satisfactory. To avoid increasing the risk or for any other reason if journals librarian prefers to postpone payment towards renewal of journals, he will risk the danger of non-supply of initial issues of the journal for the next year/volume. Further, when renewal payments are sent the back issues of the journal for which library has paid may not be available. So the cycle restarts with non-supply and request for extension of subscription period to make good the non-supply or refund towards non-supplies. This also leads to the problem of not having common expiry date for all journals of at least a given publisher. In any case libraries prefer an uninterrupted service than mere extension of subscription or receiving refunds.

9.4 Unconfirmed Prices, Additional/Supplementary Invoices and Combined Issues/Volumes

If subscription or renewal to a journal has to be paid 6-8 weeks in advance of publication, ordering and invoicing for it should take place 12-15 weeks in advance. Unfortunately many publishers would not have decided on their prices for the next year so early. As a result, invoices are not received well in time from publishers, but a reply that invoices will be sent soon after deciding the price. However, agents try to counter this problem by invoicing at unconfirmed prices and in most of the cases based on previous year's price. This invariably leads to submission and processing of additional invoices to claim the balance amount based on revised subscription rate. This not only takes for granted that library has to subscribe to the journal at whatever the revised price is but also affects budget and expenditure planning where escalations are substantial. Additional invoices may also be submitted by agents, in case of changes in conversion rates of GOC.

Additional or supplementary invoices are also sent throughout the year in some cases if publishers decide to publish additional volumes during the year. Additional expenditure for a given journal due to increase in price, escalation in conversion rates and publication of additional volumes cannot be easily avoided by a library once committed to a journal. The magnitude of the problem can be realised if one notes that, on an average, price of a journal (especially commercially published journal) is increased by about 20 per cent a year and currencies like Sterling Pound has doubled its value against Indian Rupee in last couple of years.

On the other hand, it is not uncommon to see situations where after collecting subscription to a journal, a publisher may not publish one or more issues of the journal or publish one or more combined issues/volumes for the price already paid.

Subscribing directly with publishers do not solve the problem and help in getting a single invoice. With some publishers it is necessary to remind and follow-up with extensive correspondence to get invoices. Many times what a library gets is not invoice but some scribbling on the order letter of the library without much clarity on price and other charges. Publishers normally do not honour typical Indian style subscription/renewal orders nor they have any system of sending invoice on printed proforma letter in triplicate or quadruplicate. The library and the accounts department of the organisation have to inevitably accept scribbling of publishers on library's order letter as invoice. There are examples of erratic invoicing by publishers and the same take substantial time to get resolved.

The ideal for a library is to receive well in time single preprinted proforma invoice clearly indicating price, postage, if any, the volume number and number of issues expected to be published, conversion rate, etc. for all the titles of a publisher. In fact, it is here that libraries can substantially unload their burden of correspondence on a reliable and efficient agent, if any. Certain clarifications which a library fails to get from publishers could be partly solved if agent is already subscribing to the same journal for other libraries.

Finally, if payment to a journal is made very late, some initial issues of the journal would have been out of stock. Occasionally, publishers treat such orders where payments are received in the mid of the year as order for back volumes and demand a separate back volume price.

9.5 Problems of Resource Sharing

In spite of the fact that by very nature special libraries are located in an isolated way with unique features, they are driven together more and more with resource sharing considerations mainly due to heavy escalation in prices of information resources and almost inelastic budgets. Yet resource sharing in this country is much less practiced than said in the professional gatherings. Apart from idiosyncrasies and styles of functioning of each special library and policies and practices of parent institutions, the profession as such has not made honest attempts to facilitate resource sharing among libraries and to determine, appreciate and respect factors which militate against resource sharing philosophy. Even the libraries which assume leadership in resource sharing arrangements, as far as journal subscription is concerned, do not put efforts to regularly make the list of journals subscribed and updated journal holdings widely to other libraries intending to participate and practice resource sharing. Inter library cooperation, as such, is covertly based on inter library threat and buck passing than honest efforts and mutual trust. It is extremely easy for a library to cancel ten journals and request another library to regularly supply xerox copies of content pages of issues of those journals as and when received, copies of articles as and when requested or arranging to send the issues for a short display but the effect of the same on the lending library if the requesting library does not reciprocate the same to the lending library has to be seen. What is the fate of users of a neighbouring library, where rightful primary members/users of a library are themselves are not efficiently served?

An examination of past research regarding use of information, clearly throws light on factors which act against the practice of resource sharing. It has been well established that apart from initiative of users and availability of a source of information, accessibility, ease of use, perceived utility and distance of a source of information (neighbouring library in this case) very much determine how much trouble a user is prepared to take in using a journal subscribed by another library or how long he can sustain his interest till his 'primary library' gets it on inter-library-loan for him to use in his own work place. All these factors, are bound by Mooers' law (1960, p. ii) which states that 'users will utilise an information service only when doing so costs them less than not using it.'

Further, there is a limit or break-even point for number of users who can share a journal. If there are a number of users interested in a given journal, particularly news oriented weekly journal, for all of them to have a glimpse of an issue within a week is practically impossible and the library is forced to subscribe to second copy of the same. If the library has a practice of circulating journals among interested/potential users, then it would be difficult to make it available to other libraries. The journals which can be shared with users of other libraries are those which are monthly or quarterly specialised journals and required by a limited number of users of the lending-library.

Lastly, sincere efforts to resource sharing become difficult to a library which is already overburdened with serving its own rightful users. In such situations extensive one sided inter-library requests ('resource rape') look like buck passing unless the library is formally identified for the purpose.

Looking from the angle of a special library, resource sharing arrangements in the country do not give any confidence to face budgetary problems and cancel subscription to some existing journals. Yet, as an inevitable way, one needs to find ways of informal arrangements with neighbouring libraries and take note of journals already subscribed by them before cancelling journals in one's library.

9.6 Problems of Unwanted Duplicate Issues of Journals

The policy of publishers that claims regarding missing issues be made within 60-90 days often results in over-cautious actions of sending reminders even when the issues are in transit. The result is huge accumulation of unwanted duplicate issues of journals. Libraries prefer to err on the side of getting a duplicate issue rather than missing an issue not only to serve their users and to make the volume and holdings complete but also to avoid embarrassing audit queries on missing issues. Duplicate issues of journals also keep arriving in libraries when publisher has forgotten to change mail label and subscription period. In fact, the cost of duplicate issues accumulated in a library is much higher than the cost of missing issues and transit loss, if any.

Having accumulated huge collection of duplicate issues of journals over years the problem of proper maintenance and disposal costs heavily to libraries in terms of time, efforts and space. Many libraries take a conservative attitude of maintaining such duplicate issues of journals till the original issues are bound in proper sequence so that if some issue is misplaced or lost, the duplicate issues in the collection can be profitably used. But the chances of issues that are lost are same as duplicate issues available with the library are very bleak. These duplicate issues can also be used as additional copies for circulation if the demand is high. Further, if there are departmental or local libraries within the organisation, duplicate issues of journals can be sent to them if they desire. They can also be used for exchanging with other cooperating libraries or sold if the procedure and law permit. Unfortunately there is no formal program like USBE and DEU in India to deposit duplicate issues of journals and obtain missing issues from the large stock of such cooperating agencies. One of the most important ways of disposing duplicate issues of journals is offering them to publisher/supplier or their customers within the country as a token of gesture and as a moral duty for having received a duplicate issue from them. This method in addition to adding clerical work of correspondence, at times, results in incurring substantial foreign postage where publishers insist on sending duplicate issues to them and occasionally may cause publisher to disturb regular mailing to the library. Whatever is the procedure adopted for disposal of duplicate issues of journals, it involves correspondence, recording and proper maintenance unless a formal collective arrangement is made among the cooperating libraries.

An issue very close to the issue of accumulation and disposal of duplicate issues of journals is maintenance and disposal of stray issues, sample issues and issues of free journals. Sample and stray issues of many journals may come to libraries directly from publishers, agents or users. However, libraries need to be very careful about accepting free journals. One should make sure the intentions of a publisher sending a free journal. It may be as part of propaganda or a means of publicity for products or a market strategy for a new journal. Some journals are free only to individuals. Special libraries should politely refuse such unsought free journals if on the *prima facie* they are not relevant. They need to accept free journals, if they are likely to be useful, with the condition that such journals may be discarded or sold or exchanged to other journals by the library at a later date.

What has been discussed in this chapter is only some important issues relating to journal subscription in special libraries. The usual problems of journal subscription like ever increasing number, variety and price are not dealt in detail here. There are books on serials and journals with more detailed treatment.

9.7 Cost Benefit Analysis of Journals: A Case Study

The McGraw-Hill encyclopaedia of professional management defines cost-benefit analysis (CBA) as determining ". . . the ratio of the benefits of a given project to its cost, taking into account the benefits and costs that cannot be directly measured in Dollars" (Bittel ed. 1978, p. 242). A closely related concept of cost-effectiveness analysis (CEA) ". . . is defined as a way of finding the least expensive means of reaching an objective or a way of obtaining the greatest possible value from a given expenditure" (Bittel ed. 1978, p. 242). Either to arrive at a benefit to cost ratio of a single project or to assess relatively the effectiveness of different projects, the identification and pertinent measure of all the costs and benefits of projects on identical scale of measure (e.g., dollars or rupees) is necessary. While CBA seeks to develop standards and criteria for determining how well the existing services of a library meet the requirements of its users, CEA aims at discovering new, improved procedures and devices for providing better services to the users (Leimicuhler, 1978). CBA has been considered as a valuable tool for increasing people's awareness of the costs and benefits of information and documentation as a production factor and to provide better basis for budgeting and strategic planning (Lungberg, et al., 1976).

Libraries are largely service oriented paternalistic systems and are not susceptible to precise quantitative assessment. The cost of establishing and running a library can be estimated, but how does one measure its intangible benefits? In the past, mixed reactions have greeted the use of CBA in Librarianship in general and in dealing with journals in particular. Yet, the need for CBA in libraries has been stressed by many (White, 1979; Leimikuhler, 1978). Though a substantial amount of literature has been brought out on CBA, very little has been done to demonstrate the use of CBA in libraries.[1]

Wills and Oldman (1977) reviewing some cost-benefit studies of libraries, question the assumption that "use" equals "value", and criticise the use of CBA for two reasons: (1) economic analysis is inappropriate where decisions have to be based on political factors (2) it is essential to explore how information supplied by libraries is used. Jenson (1978) also concludes that the CBA is not applicable in assessing library service. The upper hand of noneconomic considerations (Sridhar, 1985) in decision-making in libraries has been stressed by Raffel (1974), who says that the more critical the decision, the less useful a CBA to library decision-makers.

The numerous use studies of libraries have never attempted to measure "utility" or "value" (it is almost impossible to measure precisely the utility of a document or a library) but have made certain assumptions about the operational definition of "use" of a document. Francis (1976) for example, finds an absence of costing standards and suggests that many problems exist in translating the statistics of book circulation into equivalent social benefits.

Apart from exploring the difficulties of applying CBA to journals, it is attempted here to relate the subscription cost of a journal issue to its "use" during the first three months after its arrival. Kent's definition of "use" as physical selection and the act of leafing through pages of journal was adopted for the purpose (Kent, et al., 1979, p. 61). Incidentally, the "cost per use" of a journal appears to be a useful figure both in ratio analysis (Sridhar, 1986) in libraries and in ranking journals in decreasing order of cost per use.

Given a fixed budget, a library has to allocate its funds judiciously to various activities and services, while at the same time ensuring that it maximises benefit to cost ratio. In other words, libraries do carry out benefit-maximising and cost-minimising programmes. For example, if the cost of maintaining an old bound journal is much higher than borrowing it from other libraries, the library may opt to weed it out. Similarly, if in-house reprographic or micrographic work is costlier than having this work done on the outside, the library may decide to go outside for it. These are traditional make or buy decisions, and they are often, influenced by noneconomic considerations.

Much has been written about cost minimising efforts in dealing with journals. Use studies, bibliometric studies, cost-benefit studies, cost-effectiveness studies, citation studies, etc., are common. All such studies have directly or indirectly attempted to rank journals subscribed to by a library (or published in a particular field) in decreasing order of productivity, "utility" or "use". In the process, assumptions are sometimes made with little attempt to isolate factors/variables that affect both the cost of the journals and the benefit they provide. A sort of straight relation between cost and benefit may be brought forth on the assumption that other factors remain constant. Such a ranked list of journals is supposed to be used, depending upon availability of funds, in making borrow or buy decisions.

Robertson and Hansman (1979) felt that the traditional Bradford approach to bibliographic scatter involving ranking of journals according to productivity must be modified in order to answer more directly questions concerning the cost-effectiveness or cost-benefit of journal acquisition. The results obtained in using the Bradford analysis alone appeared to them to depend upon the particular journals that contribute to a field.

As far as cost-benefit analysis of journals is considered, Byrd and Koenig (1978) have pleaded for an objective cost-benefit ratio for each serial title. They point to an unfortunate situation in which selection is often based on user opinion. In addition to subscription cost, they considered many other factors in assessing values. These included coverage, impact factor, use, location, inter-library loan requests, etc. Similarly, a model for selection of journals titles based on cost-benefit ratios was developed by Kraft and Polacsek (1978), who analysed factors such as usage, relevance and availability of a title elsewhere.

Kent's study at the University of Pittsburgh was another major study in which use of books and journals was related to cost of their acquisition and maintenance (Kent et al., 1979). But controversy arose concerning implementation of the findings of this report (University of Pittsburgh, 1979).

In late 1983 a use study of current journals by Indian space technologists was carried out (Sridhar, 1986). As part of the study in-house use as well as lentout use of two latest issues of 485 current journals subscribed to by ISAC Library were monitored and recorded over three months from the date of their arrival and display in the library. For the purpose of applying CBA to journals, the use data of this study has been extracted in the case of about 6 per cent of the titles. The actual sample was picked by selecting every 15th title from the list of current journals arranged alphabetically by title. Thus, this study is restricted to a sample of 33 titles. The purpose of the study was to see how effective the CBA of journals is in a special library, to determine how the findings of CBA of journals differ from those of a simple use study and to assess how far other factors influence the decision to retain an item or not, based on its CBA. The subscription cost of the sample journals in rupees for the year 1983 as well as their periodicity have been noted to determine cost per issue. The sample journals are analysed and compared for their cost per use.

Table 9.1 provides the data on 33 sample journals subscribed to by ISAC library in terms of title, periodicity, subscription cost, use and cost per use. As already mentioned, the use data in the table is extracted from an earlier use study of current journals (Sridhar, 1986). The intention here is to extend the analysis done in the use study by incorporating the cost component and assessing to what extent the findings and recommendations of the use study hold good in the CBA. It is intended also to see whether or not further clues are provided by CBA in assessing the relative worth of a journal for a given library.

TABLE 9.1: Cost per Use of Selected Journals Subscribed to by ISAC Library

Sl. No.	Title	Periodicity	Subscription cost in Rs. per year	Cost per single issue in Rs.	Use of two issues in first 3 months	Cost per use per issue for first 3 months
1	2	3	4	5	6	7
1.	Acta Astronautica	M	4545	378.75	29	26.12
2.	Applied Mechanics Reviews	M	3636	303.00	11	55.09
3.	Astronomy and Astrophysics	F	7948	[illegible]	11	55.58
4.	Aviation Week and Space Technology	W	667	12.83	43	00.60

(*Contd.*)

TABLE 9.1 (*Contd.*)

1	2	3	4	5	6	7
5.	Celestial Mechanics	8/Yr	750	93.75	17	11.03
6.	Control Engineering	M	707	58.92	29	4.06
7.	Defense Electronics	M	364	30.33	22	2.76
8.	Electrical Communication	M	82	6.83	12	1.14
9.	Electronics and Communications in Japan	M	4245	353.75	10	70.75
10.	Energy	B M	2828	471.33	0	N A
11.	Hydraulics and Pneumatics	M	505	42.08	5	16.83
12.	IEE Proceedings. B: Electrical Power Applications	B M	5298	883.00	6	294.33
13.	IEEE Trans. on Biomedical Engineering	M	1197	99.75	8	24.94
14.	IEEE Trans. On Engineering Management	Q	364	91.00	10	18.20
15.	IEEE Trans. on Plasma Science	Q	545	136.25	7	32.43
16.	International Journal of Control	M	3227	268.92	8	67.23
17.	Journal of Applied Photographic Engineering	Q	808	202.00	2	202.00
18.	Journal of Engineering Physics	M	5383	448.58	2	448.58
19.	Journal of Photographic Science	B M	587	97.83	0	N A
20.	Journal of the Acoustic Society of America	M	1869	155.75	3	103.83
21.	Journal of the Optical Society of America	M	1818	151.50	7	43.29
22.	Machine Design	F	505	19.42	24	1.62
23.	Microelectronics and Reliability	B M	2172	362.00	34	21.29
24.	Nature	W	2820	54.23	38	2.85
25.	Optics Communication	M	3648	304.00	13	46.77
26.	Plating and Surface Finishing	M	404	33.67	6	11.22
27.	Radio and Electronic Engineer	M	885	73.75	10	14.75
28.	Satellite Communication	M	151	12.58	52	0.48
29.	SIAM Journal on Control and Optimisation	B M	889	148.17	7	42.33
30.	Solar Physics	8/Yr	6779	847.38	15	112.98
31.	Space World	10/Yr	167	16.70	21	1.15
32.	Telecommunication Journal of Australia	3/Yr	198	66.00	1	132.00
33.	Wireless World	M	277	23.08	29	1.59

Key: NA — Not Applicable; M — Monthly; F — Fortnightly; W — Weekly; Yr — Year; BM — Bimonthly; Q — Quarterly.

Note: 1. Average use per journal issue for first quarter is $\left(\frac{492}{66}=\right)$ 7.5.

2. Average cost of an issue of journal is Rs. $\left(\frac{66268}{431}=\right)$ 153.75.

3. The average cost per use of single issue in first quarter is Rs. $\left(\frac{2\times 33}{492}\times 153.75=\right)$ 20.63.

It may be noted from the table that the average use per issue of a journal (in the sample) during the first three months of its arrival and display in the ISAC Library is 7.5. The average subscription cost of an issue of a journal in the sample is Rs. 153.75 and the average cost per use of a single issue over the three months is Rs. 20.63.

As the journals *Energy* and the *Journal of Photographic Science* were not used during the sample use study, their cost per use is not worked out in Table 9.1, and hence they are excluded from the CBA. Incidentally, these are 2 of the 60 unused journals at ISAC library recommended for cancellation in the use study. In addition, there were another 34 marginally used titles (used once or twice during the first three months of their arrival) suggested for cancellation. The sample list of journals in Table 9.1 contains three such marginally used titles: the *Journal of Applied Photographic Engineering,* the *Journal of Engineering Physics* and the *Telecommunication Journal of Australia.*

On the other hand, it was recommended that 28 heavily used journals (used more than 30 times during the course of the use study) be obtained by airmail subscription and/or additional copy(ies) be subscribed to. Four of them, namely, *Aviation Week and Space Technology, Microelectronics and Reliability, Nature* and *Satellite Communication* occur in Table 9.1.

Table 9.2 presents the sample journals (31 titles, ignoring 2 that were unused) in increasing order of their cost per use. In addition, their respective ranks as per decreasing order of use and increasing order of cost are also indicated in the table. It is interesting to note that the rank order of these journals by cost per use correlates fairly highly with the rank order by use per issue as well as rank order by cost per issue. The respective values of the Spearman Rank order correlation coefficient are 0.70 and 0.85 at 0.005 significance level which indicate that as much as 70 per cent of the result of CBA is affected by the use data (i.e., benefits) and 85 per cent of the result by cost data.

An examination of Table 9.2 reveals that the news oriented popular journals score low in cost per use. For example, *Satellite Communication* received the lowest cost per use of Rs. 0.48. This is followed by *Aviation Week and Space Technology* (Rs. 0.60), *Electrical Communication* (Rs. 1.14), *Space World* (Rs. 1.15), *Wireless World* (Rs. 1.59), *Machine Design* (Rs. 1.62), *Defense Electronics* (Rs. 2.76), *Nature* (Rs. 2.85) and *Control Engineering*(Rs. 4.06). Of four heavily used journals (used more than 30 times), three have the lowest scores in cost per use. The journal *Microelectronics and Reliability*, though used heavily, scores a moderate Rs. 21.29 per use because of its relatively high subscription cost. Hence, it would not be proper to recommend airmail subscription and/or subscribing to an additional copy in its case. The journal *Electrical Communication*, which had a quite low use score (12), is at the top of the list as a result of its low cost. In other words, it has a low cost/low use profile.

TABLE 9.2: Ranked List of Journals by Cost Per Use

Rank in increasing order of cost per use	Title	Rank in decreasing order of use	Rank in increasing order of cost per issue
1	2	3	4
1 (0.48)	Satellite Communication	1 (52)	2 (12.58)
2 (0.60)	Aviation Week and Space Technology	2 (43)	3 (12.83)
3 (0.14)	Electrical Communication	14 (12)	1 (6.83)
4 (1.15)	Space World	10 (21)	4 (16.70)
5 (1.59)	Wireless World	6 (29)	6 (23.08)
6 (1.62)	Machine Design	8 (24)	5 (19.42)
7 (2.76)	Defense Electronics	9 (22)	7 (30.33)
8 (2.85)	Nature	3 (38)	10 (54.23)
9 (4.06)	Control Engineering	6 (29)	11 (58.92)
10 (11.03)	Celestial Mechanics	11 (17)	15 (93.75)
11 (11.22)	Plating and Surface Finishing	25.5 (6)	8 (33.67)
12 (14.75)	Radio and Electronic Engineer	18 (10)	13 (73.75)
13 (16.83)	Hydraulics and Pneumatics	27 (5)	9 (42.08)
14 (18.20)	IEEE Trans. on Engineering Management	18 (10)	14 (91.00)
15 (21.29)	Microelectronics and Reliability	4 (34)	27 (362.00)
16 (24.94)	IEEE Trans. on Biomedical Engineering	20.5 (8)	16 (99.75)
17 (26.12)	Acta Astronautica	6 (29)	28 (378.75)
18 (32.43)	IEEE Trans. on Plasma Science	23 (7)	17 (136.25)
19 (42.33)	SIAM Journal on Control and Optimisation	23 (7)	18 (148.17)
20 (42.29)	Journal of the Optical Society of America	23 (7)	19 (151.50)
21 (46.77)	Optics Communication	13 (13)	24 (304.00)
22 (55.09)	Applied Mechanics Review	15.5 (11)	23 (303.00)
23 (55.58)	Astronomy and Astrophysics	15.5 (11)	25 (305.69)
24 (67.23)	International Journal of Control	20.5 (8)	22 (268.92)
25 (70.75)	Electronics and Communication in Japan	18 (10)	26 (353.75)
26 (103.83)	Journal of the Acoustic Society of America	28 (3)	20 (155.75)

(*Contd.*)

TABLE 9.2 (*Contd.*)

1	2	3	4
27 (112.98)	Solar Physics	12 (15)	30 (847.38)
28 (132.00)	Telecommunication Journal of Australia	31 (1)	12 (66.00)
29 (202.00)	Journal of Applied Photographic Engineering	29.5 (2)	21 (202.00)
30 (294.33)	IEE Proceedings B: Electrical Power Applications	25.5 (6)	31 (883.00)
31 (448.58)	Journal of Engineering Physics	29.5 (2)	29 (448.58)

Note: The Spearman Rank Order Correlation Coefficient between two rankings of journals as per cost per use and use per issue is $\left(r_s = 1 - \frac{6 \times \sum Di^2}{n(n^2-1)} =\right)$ 0.7068. The *t*-test value based on $t = r_s\sqrt{\frac{n-2}{1-r_s^2}}$ is 5.3805. By looking at the tabulated value of *t*, it is found that correlation is statistically significant at 0.005. Similarly, The correlation coefficient between ranking of journals as per cost per use and cost per issue is 0.854 at 0.005 significance level.

On the other hand, the highest cost per use of Rs. 448.58 is scored by the *Journal of Engineering Physics*. Next in linc are: the *IEE Proceedings B: Electrical Power Applications* (Rs. 294.33), the *Journal of Applied Photographic Engineering* (Rs. 202.00), the *Telecommunication Journal of Australia* (Rs. 132.00), *Solar Physics* (Rs. 112.98) and the *Journal of the Acoustic Society of America* (Rs. 112.98). Interestingly, all three of the marginally used (used once or twice during the sample use study) titles mentioned earlier are included in the high cost per use group. In addition, another 3 journals, namely the *IEE Proceedings B: Electrical Power Applications, Solar Physics* and the *Journal of the Acoustic Society of America*, have also become cost ineffective because of their exorbitant subscription cost. It is these high cost per use journals that should be considered for cancellation and alternative arrangements, such as the buying of xerox copies of relevant articles made. All six of the high cost per use (> Rs. 100.00) journals are specialised journals dealing with a specific aspect of a subject and are relatively high-priced.

The findings of the journal use study were put before a representative user body for a final decision on cancellation of unused and least used journals and for a decision regarding additional copies and/or airmail subscription in the case of heavily used journals. Not all of the journals recommended for cancellation were actually cancelled. Nearly half were retained on the plea of subject specialists. In very few cases was the airmail/second copy arrangement approved. The cost dimension added to the use study has nevertheless substantially influenced the decision-makers in cutting down the number of highly priced subscriptions. An exception occurs only in the case of a few specialised journals.

Another factor considered was the nature of journals. For example, most of the local (Indian) journals were not only cheaper but also were demanded as a means of supporting the indigenous publishing efforts.

Two further considerations were taken into account. One had to do with whether a journal is published by a professional body or by a commercial publisher. Normally journals published by professional bodies are lower in subscription cost than are those published by commercial publishers. The second consideration dealt with whether a journal is a news/current-awareness journal meant for generalists or one that deals with a subject of interest primarily to specialists.

CBA is helpful in furthering the findings of the use study by grouping the journals of a library into four profiles, as depicted in the Fig. 9.1 given below:

		COST	
		Low	High
USE	Low	1	4
	High	2	3

FIG. 9.1: Four Profiles of Journals

Cell 1: Low cost and low use journals. A library does not mind having such journals as long as they are not creating an abnormal maintenance cost. Alternatively, as long as they are not to be kept in the library for a long time, they are desirable.

Cell 2: Low cost and high use journals. These are the ideal journals from a CBA angle for any library.

Cell 3: High cost and high use journals. These need a separate ranking to see whether or not some with a very high cost per use can be cancelled and xerox copies of needed articles acquired and whether or not the journal can be shared with local cooperating libraries.

Cell 4: High cost and low use journals. These need to be carefully considered for cancellation. Strong user opinion and noneconomic considerations need to be given attention.

NOTE

1. Some attempts to apply CBA to certain areas of library works like library unionisation and networking, union catalogue, electronic security system, catalogue automation, library automation network, catalogue system, library delivery systems, manpower planning, etc., have already been made.

10

SUMMARY AND CONCLUSION

It is said that an elegant library building is a white elephant unless it houses materials appropriate for its users (Spiller, 1980, p. 15). Collection development in a special library is an important preparatory work accounting for nearly two-thirds of its operational expenses and space (Buckland, 1989) and has strong effect on efficiency and effectiveness of its services. Collection development policy should take into account the degree to which material has to be borrowed from other libraries. There are a number of problems in collection development: many are common and few are unique to the library concerned. Judicial and scientific assessment of problems is bound to reveal options open to special libraries. Value judgment of practitioners alone is not adequate.

It is possible to develop demand forecasting techniques for libraries on par with those in industry as described in Chapter 2. But the efforts and expertise needed are rarely deployed for the purpose. As discussed earlier there is no single ideal method of demand forecasting suitable for all situations. It obviously depends on types and levels of users and information, availability of data, time and funds. In practice, one has to make wise decision in choosing a suitable method. A combination of two or more methods is often desirable when they can supplement and check each other. Whatever the technique, in all cases, one should bear in mind that the approach should be a unified approach of expertise and technique.

Most of the results of information-need/requirement studies (presented in Chapter 2) are either speculative or theoretical in nature and are not supported by a rigorous analysis of hard data. Past studies have not addressed the information-needs and requirements of under-privileged and deprived users, less frequent users and non-users (Ford, 1977, p. 20). In the case study of information requirements of the space technologists presented in Chapter 2, the requirements of S&T news and basic S&T information have ranked high for the space technologists . In addition, the space technologists seek more of theoretical background, experimental results, methods, processes and procedures, product, material, equipment and apparatus information and physical, technical and design data (in that rank order) than state-of-the-art, review literature, standard and patent specifications. Information is sought only when it is utmost needed and there is a strong need for internally generated information and product information. Different types of information are used intermittently in an intermixed way by the space technologists depending on the nature of work. Change in the nature of work of the space technologists is found to affect both the intensity and the type of information needed. The problem of 'information overload', enlargement of boundaries of interest and intensification of space activities in the country, impact of electronics boom and resultant need for condensed information-services and the need for fast serving information intermediaries or agents are felt by the space technologists.

A case study of user-participation in collection development presented in Chapter 3 revealed rather low participation of users in collection development of the Library. Though some of the possible reasons attributable to such low participation of users have been identified through informal discussions with them, it would be worthwhile to undertake a separate study to bring out clearly the reasons for such apathy, so as to evolve measures to motivate more and more users to involve themselves actively in the process of collection development that would reflect their potential interest. Some suggestions to improve user-participation in collection development presented in the Chapter also require further study. It is also highly desirable to find out how the documents suggested by users are later used by the users. Analysing the use pattern of library collection after a given number of years of acquiring them not only reveals the relative strengths and weaknesses of collection developed, but also helps in detecting shallow collection development policies, if any.

In the light of a number of peculiar problems of document acquisition enumerated in Chapter 4 it would not be wrong if one says that a sort of blind man's choice takes place in document acquisition without really knowing how much is being paid for how much of utility of the product. Document acquisition in libraries calls for a business oriented approach. It is a continuous activity where changes in book trade, and other environmental factors have to be taken into account in addition to continuous monitoring and evaluation of existing suppliers, vigilant look out for alternate sources of supply and opportunity for efficient and economic acquisition. In addition, acquisitions librarian has to keep an eye on what collection he has, its strength and weakness, how it is being used and what changes in the requirements of users are anticipated to suitably modify the document acquisition programme. In other words, acquisitions librarian has to involve himself in all the phases of collection management and evaluation.

The case study of user-participation in collection development (Chapter 3) is further extended to enumerate the problems of document procurement delays and how such delays act as demotivator to user-participation in collection development in Chapter 5. How much time the Library has taken to acquire the items suggested by users is also examined. To recapitulate from the analysis (Chapter 5), out of 818 on-demand books ordered during 1983 only 426 (52%) were supplied by September 1984, and average supplying efficiency of exclusive/specialised Indian dealers, foreign vendors and Indian vendors were 82 per cent, 59 per cent and 28 per cent respectively. The direct orders on publishers and miscellaneous suppliers have brought reasonably good supplies. The cumulative percentage of books supplied is not directly proportional to time in case of Indian vendors. The study indicated that among the Indian vendors IS6, IS8 and IS11 were more efficient than others. With mushrooming of retail book vendors and certain problems of the trade no sign of improvement in supply position of on-demand books is seen in the near future. They try to concentrate on fairly costly books, standing orders on serials, books of popular publishers and prefer dealer library (approval) plan to promote what is available (or what is left?) in their stock than meeting on-demand requirements of users. Very few of them have systematic method of informing libraries about status of pending supplies to enable libraries to take alternate action. In this respect, foreign vendors are quite prompt. With their computerised system, they inform libraries about status of supply as well as cancel pending orders after lapse of stipulated period. Few years ago, a similar experiment was done by ISAC Library with Indian wholesale dealers and the result was not much different from that of Indian retail vendors.

If user-participation in collection development is discouraging, the supplying efficiency is much more gloomy as discussed in Chapter 5, thereby creating a vicious circle in special libraries where users are conscious of their rights and sensitive about their demands. Users loose faith in indenting/suggesting books to library if their earlier indents are not yet been fulfilled. Even after discounting an element of subjectivity in their feelings, there is truth in their views as evidenced in the case study presented in Chapter 5.

If a library wishes to have constant patronage and participation of users in collection development, newer methods such as obtaining by bulk air freight and/or selective airmail from foreign vendors may have to be explored at least in case of on-demand books once convinced about non-availability in local market. Knowing where a library stands in terms of procurement of on-demand books and using the results to frame future procurement policies are necessary. Since users are not much concerned with the problems faced by libraries with the book trade/suppliers all the delays have to be apparently absorbed as delays at libraries and the acquisitions librarians have to smilingly say 'user is always right'. The problem of procurement delays persists to a great extent.

A case study of collection development of technical reports in a satellite technology library presented in Chapter 6 showed the importance of gray literature in certain high technology areas. The unusual problems of negative and excess bibliographic control, duplication among reports announcement bulletins, problems in eliminating duplication in collection, poor physical getup and conditions of reports, excessive application of security classification and abundant number of internally generated reports are some of the unique problems of technical reports in special libraries. It was also seen in Chapter 6 that the process of choosing an appropriate vendor/supplier for reports is to be based on economy, efficiency (as reflected in supply position of sample orders of a library), effectiveness and informativeness and readiness of suppliers to respond to queries of libraries. The last consideration is qualitative involving value judgment and the risk of subjectivity. Also this criterion is not normally applicable to foreign agents and direct supply sources as they give less attention for such correspondence. However, having located far away from major agencies such as NTIS (whose service cannot be availed without sufficient clarifications) one need to increasingly depend on Indian agents for choosing and availing services of NTIS. The problems of procurement of technical reports (Chapter 6) has once again revealed that as market conditions change, libraries need to suitably modify their procurement policies.

Microforms are versatile, economic and efficient information handling media without which no library of present day can hope for comprehensive collection development. It was seen in Chapter 7 that one of the important aspects in developing micrographics in special libraries is to consider it as a system. It is very necessary to identify relation of micrographics with other systems such as reprographics, automation, etc. Before proceeding further, one should ascertain the nature of existing collection and facilities within the library and also at various departments within the organisation, if any. The most crucial aspects involved relate to deciding on formats, types, reduction ratios and sources of procurement of microforms. Organisation, maintenance, quality control and inspection of microforms, selection of user-aid equipments, preventive measures regarding work hazards in micrographics, design of furniture for micrographics, layout for micrographics unit, copyright problems relating to micrographics, etc., which are not covered in these pages also need to be considered in developing micrographics collection in a special library. As far as situation in India is concerned there are no micropublishers in the country. However, there are agencies and organisations which can produce microforms from hard copies. Most of them cover only traditional formats such as films, jackets and rarely fiches. At present, special libraries are acquiring microforms mostly from suppliers abroad. Very few libraries are going for converting existing collection to microform. In the areas of user-aid equipments, except few readers, nothing else, not even good quality storing and maintenance equipments are locally available. The industry is yet to develop adequate indigenous equipments to promote use of microforms.

It is suggested that unified professional efforts have to be put in to develop and establish good micrographics facilities to make microforms more popular among users. In this direction an updated data bank of evaluated information about indigenous as well as imported micrographics equipment should be made available by national information and documentation centres and micrographics associations. Professional journals in the country should devote at least one column for exchange of information about new micrographics equipment and facilities among Indian libraries.

Evaluation reports about new equipment manufactured in the country and those imported should be regularly brought out by competent experts and associations. More facilities either commercial or from government institutions are needed for getting hard copies of microform documents.

There are a number of advantages and disadvantages of vendor controlled order plans like blanket/standing/bulk orders, dealer library plan, membership packages and other similar ways of acquiring documents (Chapter 8). Such methods have to be fully explored by acquisitions librarians with an assessment through cost benefit analysis. It was revealed in the case study of standing order for NASA reports (in Chapter 8) that there are different ways (decision theory methods) of assessing such orders and a decision maker has to be provided with different alternatives. Finally the non-economic considerations of the decision cannot be underestimated.

The problems of journal subscription are the most complex and peculiar to any library (Chapter 9). Choosing an agent, taking risk in huge advance payments, handling irregularity in supplies, transit losses, getting extension of subscription period or refund for non-supplies, checking prices, handling unconfirmed prices and supplementary invoices, promoting resource sharing, disposal of duplicate and stray issues of journals, etc. are some of the important problems of journal subscription. Quite a few of the problems evade solutions and some cannot be generalised to all libraries. Diverse opinions and experiences have been aired by professional colleagues and experts on these issues.

It was concluded in a study that CBA may not provide a completely satisfactory solution to problems of journal retention or cancellation. It does, however, provide some clues as to how to proceed over and above those provided by a simple use study. CBA increases the awareness of librarians, administrators and users concerning collection prerogatives, but must be used in conjunction with intuitive judgement. Above all, non-economic considerations and user opinion dominate the decision-making in journal subscription.

The problems of collection development in special libraries require serious, continuous and systematic study and research by practitioners with a view to put forth better and alternative solutions. Collection development is largely neglected area of research in librarianship. Interestingly, the National Steering Committee for University Libraries of the Ministry of Education in China has offered suggestions on how to strengthen studies of collection development and identified several research topics for libraries and library staff to select and study in combination with their work and report the findings to the Secretariat for coordination (Yu, 1988, p 67-68). Simple surveys and reporting of statistics of libraries are not enough. Well designed experimental research on many problems discussed in these pages could provide some bases for decision making by practitioners when collection development problems are faced. For example, there are a number of ways of forecasting demand (Chapter 2) and their relative merits and suitability in actual practice are largely left for value judgment. To give more specific example, participation of users, staff and higher level managers in collection development continues in special libraries in varying degrees. Incidentally, they are analogous to some demand forecasting methods presented in Chapter 2. It is not clear about the relationship of use of documents and the group of people who select them. In fact a simple and small study in four institutions indicated that there was a higher percentage of use of librarian-selected material than of others (Clark, 1976, p. 122). Due to insufficient sample and lack of reinforcement of the finding in different environments, librarians have not been able to use this result with confidence.

15. M/s Gaylord Bros, Inc, TWX 710, 545-0232, Box 4901, Syracuse, N Y 13221, U S A.
16. M/s General Computing Corp, 444, Park Avenue South, N Y 10016, U S A.
17. M/s Heit Inc, Karl, 979 Third Avenue, New York, N Y 10022, U S A.
18. M/s Hitachi Limited, 5-1, Marunouchi, 1-Chome, Chiyoda-ku, Tokyo 100, Japan (*Indian Agent:* M/s Hitachi New Delhi, Liaison Office, 4th Hansalaya Building (4th Floor), 15, Barakhamba Road, New Delhi-110 001).
19. M/s Image System Inc, 11244, Playa Court, Culver City, California 90230, U S A.
20. Information Design Inc, 3247, Middlefield Road, Menlo Park, California 94025, U S A.
21. M/s Itek Business Products, Itek Corp, Rochester, N Y 14603, U S A.
22. M/s Iwatsu Electric Co, Ltd, 7-41, Kugayama, 1-Chome, Suginami Ku, Tokyo 168, Japan.
23. M/s Ixodack India Ltd, SA, Greames Road, Madras-600 006.
24. M/s Izon Corporation, 45, Research Drive, Stanford, Connecticut : 06906, U S A.
25. M/s Keuffel and Esser Co, 20, Whippnay Road, Morristown, N J 07960, U S A.
26. M/s Konishiroku Photo Ind. Co, Ltd, Shinjuku Nomura Building, 26-2, Nishi Shinjuku 1-Chome, Shinjuku Ku, Tokyo-160, Japan.
27. M/s Library Resources Inc, 301, East Eric St., Chicago, 111.60611, U S A.
28. M/s MEMCOM International, 450 E, Chapman Ave., Suite 207, Orange, California, 92666, U S A (*Indian Agent:* M/s International SIT 46, Karani Building, New Charani Road, Bombay-400 004).
29. M/s Memorex Corporation, 1180, Shulman Ave, Santa Clara, California 95052, U S A.
30. M/s Micobra Corporation, 176, King Street, P O Box 1187, Hanover, Massachussetts 02339, U S A.
31. M/s Micro Design, 857, West State Street, Hartford, Wisconsin 53027, U S A.
32. M/s Micro Display Systems, 2, Penn Plaza, New York, N Y 10001, U S A.
33. M/s Microfilm Products Inc, 40 West, 15th Street, New York, N Y 10011, U S A.
34. M/s Micro Information Systems Inc, 467, Armour Circle, N E Atlanta, Georgia 30324, U S A.
35. M/s Micro Scan Systems Inc, 54, South Main Street, Pearl River, N Y 10965, U S A.
36. M/s Minolta Camera Co, Ltd, 30, Azuchi-machi, 2-chome, Higashi-ku, Osaka 541, Japan.
37. M/s Minolta Corporation, 101, Williams Drive, Ramsey, New Jersey 07446, U S A.
38. M/s Morgan Information Systems Inc, 193, Constitution Drive, Menlo Park, California 94025, U S A.
39. M/s National Cash Register Co, Industrial Products Division, Dayton, Ohio 45409, U S A (*Indian Agent:* Cash Register Co. (India) Pvt Limited, 40, B B D Bag East, Calcutta-700 001).
40. M/s National Micrographics Systems Inc, 926, Philadelphia Avenue, Silver Spring, Maryland 20910, U S A.
41. M/s Pamtek Manufacturing Inc, 4221, Hollis Street, Oakland, California 95014, U S A.

42. M/s Quantor Corporation, 1525, Comstock, Santa Clara, California 95050, U S A.
43. M/s Rank Xerox Limited, 338, Euston Road, London, NW 3 BH, U K (*Indian Agents:* (*a*) M/s Modi Xerox Limited, Modipuram-250 110, U P, India; (*b*) No 2/1, Kasturba Road, Bangalore-560 001).
44. M/s Readex Microprint Corp., 5, Union Square, New York, N Y 10003, U S A.
45. M/s Realist Inc, N 93, W 16288, Megal Drive, Menomonee Falls, Wisconsin 53051, U S A.
46. M/s Remington Rand Office Systems Division, P O Box 171, Marietta, Ohio 45750, U S A.
47. M/s Ricoh of America, 350, Fifth Avenue, New York, N Y 10001, U S A.
48. M/s SFS Saul K G, 4898, Ronson Court, Suite F, San Diego, California, 92111, U S A.
49. M/s Sharp Corporation, 22-22, Nagaike-cho, Abeno-ku, Osaka 545, Japan.
50. M/s Stromberg Datagraphix Inc, P O Box 2449, San Diego, California 92112, U S A.
51. M/s Toshiba Corporation, 1-6, Uchi Saiwai-cho, 1-Chome, Chiyoda-ku, Tokyo 100, Japan.
52. M/s University Microfilms International, Equipment Order Department 300 N, Zeeb Road, Ann Arbor, Michigan 48106, U S A.
53. M/s Washington Scientific Industries, Longlake, Michigan 55356, U S A.
54. M/s 3M Company, Microfilm Products Division, 3M Centre, St. Paul, Minnesota 55101, U S A. (*Indian Agent:* M/s Associated Printers, (Madras) Pvt Limited, 3M Products Division, P B No 318, 165, Mount Road, Madras-600 002).
55. M/s Library Microfilms & Materials Co, 707, Augusta Street, Inglewood, California 90302, 213/678-0036, U S A.
56. M/s Information Design Inc, P O Box 2064, 3247 Middlefield Road, Menlo Park, California 94025, (415) 369-2962, U S A.
57. M/s Microphax Limited, 36, Nuffield Way, Abingdon, Oxon OX14 ITF U K.

APPENDIX III

SELECTED LIST OF SUPPLIERS

1. Books

A. *Foreign*

Baker & Taylor
50, Kirby Ave
Sommerville
NEW JERSEY 08876

Ballen Book Sellers Intl. Inc.,
125, Ricefield Lane
Hauppauge
NEW YORK 11786

Blackwell North America Inc.,
6024, SW Jean Road
Building G
Lake Oswege
OREGON 97034

Bumpus Haldane & Maxwell Limited
4, Midland Road, Olney
Bucks
MK46 4BN
UNITED KINGDOM

Felter and Simons Inc.,
100, Paik Avenue
NEW YORK NY 10017

GRH Publications
2, Wayne Close
Lowestolt Sufflok
NR32 4SX
ENGLAND

Heffers Book Sellers
20, Trinity Street
Cambridge
ENGLAND CB2 3NG

International Book Distributor Inc,
599, Industrial Avenue
Paramus
New Jersey 07652
NJ

OTO Research Corporation
Takeuchi Bldg.
1-34-12, Takatanobaba
Shinjuku-ku, Tokyo 160
JAPAN

Research Books Inc.,
38, Academy Street
P.O.Box 1507, Madison
CONNECTICUT 06443

Steward & Sons
P.O.Box 24-8583
Miami, Florida 33124
U.S.A.

Strand Book Store Inc.,
828, Broadway
NEW YORK NY 10003

World Scientific Pub. Co. Pvt. Ltd.,
Farrer Road
P.B.No. 128
SINGAPORE 9128

B. Indian

Affiliated East-West Press Pvt. Ltd.,
104, Nirmal Towers
26, Barakhamba Road
NEW DELHI 110 001

Allied Publishers
Jayadeva Hostel Building
6th Main Road
Gandhinagar
BANGALORE 560 009

Allied Publishers Pvt. Ltd.,
13/14, Asaf Ali Road
NEW DELHI 110 002

Allied Publishers Pvt. Ltd.,
15, Graham Road
Ballard Estate
BOMBAY 400 001

Asian Books Pvt. Ltd.,
7/28, Mahavir Lane,
I Floor, Ansari Road
Darya Ganj
NEW DELHI 110 002

BI Publications
54, Janpath
NEW DELHI 110 001

Business Promotion Bureau (BPB)
4794, Bharat Ram Road
23, Darya Ganj
NEW DELHI 110 002

Concept Publishing Company
23, Ansari Road
Darya Ganj
NEW DELHI 110 002

Current Tech. Literature Co. Pvt. Ltd.,
India House
Opp. G.P.O., P.B.No. 1374
BOMBAY 400 001

Current Technical Literature Co. Pvt. Ltd.,
152, Thambu Chetty Street
P.B.No. 128
MADRAS 600 001

Educational Book Centre
191, Samuel Street
P.B.No. 5148
BOMBAY 400 009

Educational Supplies
P.O.Box No. 8204
Jayanagar
BANGALORE 560 082

Galgotia Publications Pvt. Ltd.,
P.O.Box No. 7221
5 Ansari Road
NEW DELHI 110 002

Gangaram's Book Bureau
No. 72, 1st Floor
M.G. Road
BANGALORE 560 001

Higginbothams Limited
814, Anna Salai Road
MADRAS 560 002

Higginbothams Pvt. Ltd.,
74, Mahatma Gandhi Road
BANGALORE 560 002

Hind Book House
A-29, New Friends Colony
NEW DELHI 110 065

IBH Publishing Company
412, Tulsiani Chambers
Nariman Point
BOMBAY 400 021

India Book House
22, Bhulabhai Desai Road
BOMBAY 400 026

International Book Distributors
4405/2-5, Ansari Road
NEW DELHI 110 002

International Book House Pvt. Ltd.,
Indian Mercantile Mansion (Extension)
Madam Cama Road
BOMBAY 400 039

Jaico Book Distributors
G-2, 16 Ansari Road
Darya Ganj
NEW DELHI 110 002

Jaico Book House
14/1, 1st Main Road
6th Cross, Gandhinagar
BANGALORE 560 009

Informatics (I) Pvt. Ltd.,
P.B.No. 360, 87,
II Floor, 11th Cross
Malleswaram
BANGALORE 560 003

3. Standards, Patents and Reprints

A. *Foreign*

ASHRAE
1791, Tullie Circle
NE Atlanta
GEORGIA 30329-2305

British Library Document Supply Centre
Boston Spa
Wetherby, LS 237 BQ
UNITED KINGDOM

British Standards Institution
Linford Wood
Milton Keynes KM14 6LE
UNITED KINGDOM

Derwent Publications Ltd.,
Rochdale House, 128
Theobalds Road
LONDON WCIX 8RP
ENGLAND

Electronic Industries Association
2001 Eye Street
NW Washington DC 2006
U.S.A.

Engineering Information Inc.,
345, East 47th Street
NEW YORK NY 10017
U.S.A.

IEEE Service Centre
445, Hoes Lane
P.O.Box 1331
Piscataway NJ, USA
08855-1331

Information Publications Pvt. Ltd.,
Pei-Fu Industrial Bldg.
24, New Industrial Road
02 06 SINGAPORE 1953

Institute for Interconnecting & Packaging Electric Cir.
7380, North Lincoln Avenue
LINCOLNWOOD IL 60646
U.S.A.

Institution of Radio & Electronics Engineers, Australia
Commercial Unit 3
2 New Mchean Street
SYDNEY NSW 2027

International Organisation for Standardisation
1 RUC de Varembe
CP 56 1211 Geneva 20
SWITZERLAND

National Standards Association
1200, Quince Orchard Blvd
Gaithersburg MD 20878
U.S.A.

Naval Publications & Forms Center
5801, Tabor Avenue
Philadelphia PA 19120
U.S.A.

Research Publications
P.O. Box. 45, Reading
RG1 8HF
ENGLAND

B. *Indian*

Allied Publishers (P) Ltd.,
750, Mount Road,
MADRAS 600 002

Book Supply Bureau
628, 1st Main Road
1st Stage, Indiranagar
BANGALORE 560 038

Book Supply Bureau
D-44, South Extn. Part I
NEW DELHI 110 049

Bureau of Indian Standards
F Block, Unity Building
Narasimharaja Square
BANGALORE 560 002

Bureau of Indian Standards
Manok Bhavan
9, Bahadur Shah Zafar Marg
NEW DELHI 110 002

INSDOC
14, Satsang Vihar Marg
NEW DELHI 110 067

INSDOC Regional Centre
Indian Institute of Science Campus
BANGALORE 560 012

4. Journals

A. *Foreign*

Bumpus Haldane & Maxwell Limited
4, Midland Road, Olney
Bucks
MK46 4BN
UNITED KINGDOM

Faxon Company Inc.,
15, Southwest Park
Westwood
MA 02090
U.S.A.

Scientific & Technical Book Services Limited
P.O.Box 90, Reading
RG1 8JL
ENGLAND

Swets Subscription Service
P.O.Box 830
2160, SZ Lisse
THE NETHERLANDS

Quadrant Subscription Agency
G.R.D. Floor Post Room
Oakfield House,
35, Perrymount Road
West Sussex
RH163DH, ENGLAND

B. *Indian*

A&A Periodical Subscription Agency Pvt. Ltd.,
1865, Tri Nagar
DELHI 110 035

Allied Publishers Subscription Agency
13/14, Asaf Ali Road
NEW DELHI 110 002

Allied Publishers Subscription Agency
Jayadeva Hostel Building
5th Main Road, Gandhinagar
BANGALORE 560 009

Associated Subscription and Information Services
2, Viswanathan Street
MADRAS 600 033

Central News Agency Pvt. Ltd.,
23/90 Connaught Circus
NEW DELHI 110 001

Continental Subscription Agency,
55, Veerabadra Street,
Nungambakkam,
MADRAS 600 034

Creative Books & Periodicals P. Ltd.,
7, Nanabhai Lane
BOMBAY 400 001

Gandharwa Enterprises Pvt. Ltd.,
18, J.P. Market Eros
NEW DELHI 110 014

Globe Publications International Subscription Agency
C-62, Inderpuri
NEW DELHI 110 012

India Book Distributors
Mota Chambers
First Floor
9, Cunningham Road
BANGALORE 560 052

India Book House
Subscription Agency
514, Shivalaya, 174
C-IN-C Road
MADRAS 600 105

India Book House
5th Main Road
Gandhinagar
BANGALORE 560 009

Informatics (I) Pvt. Ltd.,
P.B.No. 2025
Sheshadripuram
BANGALORE 560 020

International News Agency
A-8/1, Nanda Road
Adarsh Nagar
DELHI 110 033

Journals Subscription Services
2547/7, Beadon Pura
Ajmal Khan Road
Karol Bagh
NEW DELHI 110 005

Living Media India Limited
74/1, St. Marks Road
BANGALORE 560 001

Living Media India Limited
2nd Floor, F-14/15
Connaught Place
NEW DELHI 110 001

Mahajan Brothers
Super market Basement
Near Natraj Cinema
Ashram Road
AHMEDABAD 380 009

Niharika Agency Pvt. Ltd.,
9, Palika Place
Panchkuian Road
NEW DELHI 110 001

Oriental Booksellers and Subscription Agents
18, Jangpura Market
NEW DELHI 110 014

Oxford Subscription Agency
Park Hotel Building
17, Park Street
CALCUTTA 700 016

Pads Subscription Services
6&7, Kamala Arcade
669, Anna Salai
Thousand Lights
MADRAS 600 006

Research Periodicals Organisation
1865, Tri Nagar
DELHI 110 035

Sage Publications India Pvt. Ltd.,
M-32 Market
Greater Kailash I
P.B.No. 4215
NEW DELHI 110 048

Standard Book Company
4/17, Morzaria Industrial Estate
Bannerghatta Road
BANGALORE 560 029

Universal Subscription Agency P. Ltd.,
5, Ansari Road
NEW DELHI 110 002

Universal Subscription Service
18-19, Community Centre
Saket, P.B.No. 8
NEW DELHI 110 017

BIBLIOGRAPHY

Aims, A. "Survey of information needs of physicists and chemists." *Journal of Documentation* 21(2) June 1965: 83-112.

Alem, William R. et al. "Developing a quantitative formula for the book collection in small academic technical libraries." *Science and Technology Libraries* 2(1) Fall 1981: 59-68.

American Library Association, Resources and Technical Services Division, Resources section, Collection Development Committee. "Guidelines for the formulation of collection development policies." *Library Resources and Technical Services* 21(1) Winter 1977: 40-47.

American Library Association. "Collection development policies." Chicago: American Library Association, Association of College and Research Libraries, 1981.

Arthur, Anthony. "Collection management an Australian project." *Australian Academic and Research Libraries* 17(1) March 1986: 29-38.

Ary, Herner and Saul, Herner. "The current status of the government research report in the USA." *UNESCO Bulletin for Libraries* 13(809) August-September 1959: 187-196.

Ashby, Frederic R. *Practical librarian : a manual for all those engaged in the management of small libraries* England: The author, 1974.

Aslib, Information Department. "Report literature in the UK." *Aslib Proceedings* 25(8) August 1973: 320-325.

Auerbach Corporation. DoD User Needs Study, Phase I. Final Technical Report, 2 vols. DoD 1151-TR-3; AD 615 501, 2. Philadelphia, pa.: Auerbach Corporation, 1965.

———. "What's wrong with information retrieval?" *Machine Design* 38(16) 7 July 1966: 106-109.

Auger, C.P. ed. *Use of report literature* Hamden, Conn.: Shoe string Press, 1975.

Auger, Peter. "Non-conventional literature: Chairman's introduction". *Aslib Proceedings* 34(11/12) November-December 1982: 457-458.

Avedon, Don. "The user's guide to standard microfiche formats." 3 ed. Maryland: NMA, 1976.

Axford, H. William. "Collection management : a new dimension." *Journal of Academic Librarianship* 6(6) Jan. 1981: 324-329.

Baatz, Wilmer H. "Collection development in 19 libraries of the Association of Research Libraries." *Library Acquisitions : Practice and Thoory* 2(2) 1978: 85-121.

Bastille, Jacqueline D. and Mankin, Carole J. "A simple objective method for determining a dynamic journal collection." *Bulletin of Medical Library Association* 68(4) Oct. 1980: 357-366.

Batten, W.I. *"Handbook of special librarianship and information work."* 4 ed. London: Aslib, 1975.

Baughman, James C. *Toward a structural approach to collection development.* College and Research Libraries. May 1977: 241-248.

Baughman, James C. "Toward a structural approach to collection development." *College and Research Libraries* 38(3) May 1977: 241-24.

Benning, V.J. "Reports." In: K.W. Mildren ed. Use of engineering literature. London: Butterworths, 1976: 62-75.

Betts, Douglas. "Stock management : the basis of the problem". *Bulletin des Bibliotheques de France* 32(1) 1987: 10-17.

Bittel, Lester Robert ed. *Encyclopaedia of professional management.* New York: McGraw-Hill, 1978.

Bostic, Mary J. "A written collection development policy : to have and have not." *Collection Management* 10(3/4) 1988: 89-103.

Boylan, N.T.G. "Technical reports, identification and acquisition." RQ 10 Fall 1970: 18-21.

Brearley, Neil. "The role of technical report in scientific and technical communication." *IEEE transactions on professional communication PC*-16 (3) September 1973: 117-119.

Brittain, J. Michael. "Information and its Users – A Review with Special Reference to Social Sciences." New York: Wiley Interscience, 1971.

Brown, Clara D. "Serials : acquisition and maintenance." Birmingham: EBSCO Ind. Inc., 1972.

Brown, Clara D. and Smith, Lynn S. "Serials: past, present and future" Birmingham: EBSCO Ind. Inc., 1980.

Bryant, Bonita. "The organisational structure of collection development." *Library Resources and Technical Services* 31(2) April/June 1987: 111-122.

Buckland, Michael K. "Roles of collections and the scope of collection development." *Journal of Documentation* 45(3) 1989: 213-226.

Buzzard, Marion L. and Whaley, John H. "Serials and collection development." *Drexel Library Quarterly* 21(1) Winter 1985: 37-49.

Byrd, Gary D. and Koenig, Michael E.D. "Systematic serials selection analysis in a small academic health sciences library." *Bulletin of Medical Libraries Association* 66(4) Oct. 1978: 397-406.

Calderhead, Patrica Ed. *Libraries for professional practice* London: Architectural Press, 1972.

Canada, Council of Federal Libraries, Collection rationalisation committee. *Proceedings* of a workshop on collection development and rationalisation. tele beche, 1982.

Cargill, Jennifer S. and Alley, Brian. *Practical approval plan management*. Phoenic: Oryx press, 1979.

Carpenter, Eric J. "Collection development policies based on approval plans." *Library Acquisitions: Practice and Theory* 13(1) 1989: 39-43.

Caywood, Carolyn. "Nonprint media selection guidelines." *Journal of Youth Services in Libraries* 2(1) Fall 1988: 90-94.

Cermakova, Jirina. "The report literature : production and distribution in the USA." *Annals of Library Science and Documentation* 22(1) March 1975: 12-20.

Chillag, J.P. "Problems with reports, particularly microfiche reports." *Aslib Proceedings* 22(5) May 1970: 201-206.

———. "Don't be afraid of reports." *BLL Review* 1(2) October 1973: 39-51.

Clark Jr., Robert L. *Archive-library relations* New York: R.R. Bowker Co., 1976.

Cline, Hugh F. and Sinnott, Loraine T. *Building library collections*. Lexington, Massachusetts: Lexington Books 1981.

Cole, P.F. "Analysis of reference questions records as a guide to the requirements of scientists." *Journal of Documentation* 14(4) December 1958: 197-207.

"Collection development in action." *Library Acquisitions: Practice and Theory* 13(1) 1989: 33-64.

"Collection development." *Education Libraries* 13(1) Winter 1988: 5-19.

Columbia University, Bureau of Applied Social Research. Review of Studies in the Flow of Information among Scientists (Study Director: Herbert Menzel) 2 vols. New York: Columbia University, BASR, 1960.

Conway, Suzy, et al. "Selection and acquisitions manual development." *Bulletin Medical Libraries Association* 67(1) Jan. 1979: 54-59.

Cooper, Marianne. "Collection development in science and technology : A focus on books." *Science and Technology Libraries* 3(3) Spring 1983: 15-29.

Costrigan, Daniel M. ed. "1978-79 guide to Micrographic equipments. Vol. 1 Production equipments. Vol. 2 User Equipments." 7 ed. Maryland: NMA, 1979.

Cott, Van. "National information system for psychologists : a proposed solution for a processing problem." *American Psychologist* 25(5) May 1970: i-xx.

Crissinger, John D. "The use of journal citations in theses as a collection development methodology." Keeping current with geoscience information: *Proceedings* of the 15th meeting of the Geoscience Information Society edited by N.J. Pruett. Virginia: Geoscience Information Society, 1981: 113-124.

Hanger, Stephen. "Collection development in the British Library : the role of the RLG conspectus." *Journal of Librarianship* 19(2) April 1987: 89-107.

Hanson, C.W. "Research on users' needs : where it is getting us?" *Aslib Proceedings* 16(2) February 1964: 64-78.

Harris, Colin. "User needs and user education." A paper presented at Fifth Information Officers Training Course (INFOTRAC) 6-31 May 1985, Manila, Philippines. Organised by TECHNONET ASIA and APCTT National and International Transfer and Development. N. p. n. p., 1985.

Hartas, J.C. "Government scientific and technical reports and their problems." *Assistant Librarian* 59 March 1966: 54-59.

———. "Technical report literature : its nature and some problems." In: Bernard Houghton ed. *Information work today*. London: Clive Bingley, 1967. 77-87.

Hatt, Frank, *Reading Process : A Framework for Analysis and Description* London: Clive Bingley, 1976.

Havelock, Ronald G. "Research utilization." In Manfred Kochen and Joseph C. Donhue eds. *Information for the Community*. Chicago: ALA, 1976. Chapter 13, 200-213.

Hazen, Dan C. "Modeling collection development behaviour: a preliminary statement", *Collection Management* 4(1/2) Spring/Summer 1982: 1-14.

Hazen, Dan C. "Modeling collection development behaviour : a preliminary statement." *Collection Management* 4(1-2) Spring-Summer 1982: 1-14.

Hazen, Dan C. et al. "Research library collections in a changing universe : four points of view." *College and Research Libraries* 45(3) May 1984: 214-224.

Herner, Saul and Herner, N. "Determining requirements for atomic energy information from reference questions." In: *Proceedings* of the International Conference on Scientific Information, Washington, D.C. 16-21 November 1958. Washington, D.C.: National Academy of Sciences, 1959. 1: 181-187.

Hernon, Peter and Purcell, Gary R. *Developing collections of U.S. government publications*. London: Jai Press 1982 (Foundations in library and information science vol. 12).

Hicks, Warran B. and Ahna M. Tillin. *Managing multimedia libraries*. New York: R.R. Bowker, 1977.

Ho, May Lein and Loertscher, David V. "Collection mapping : the research." *Drexel Library Quarterly* (2) Spring 1985: 22-39.

Hodowanec, George V. "Literature obsolescence, dispersion and collection development." *College and Research Libraries* 44(6) November 1983: 421 443.

Houghton, Barnard. "Technical information sources : a guide to patent specifications, standards and technical reports literature" 2 ed. Hamden, Conn.: Shoe String Press, 1972.

Houser, L. et al. "Proceedings of a workshop on collection development and rationalisation." Ottawa: Council of Federal Libraries, Collection Rationalisation Committee, 1982.

Howard, Jeanne G. "Synergy for research library collections." *Libri* 38(3) September 1988: 205-209.

ISI. Code of practice for handling and storage of microtransparencies (microfilm and microfiche). IS:3130-1972. 1973.

Jarred, Ada D. "The one minute collection manager." *Collection Management* 9(4) Winter 1987: 5-12.

Jenson, Niels. "Cost benefit and the library service just don't go together." *Bibliotek* 70(12) 1978: 310-311.

Katz, William A. "Collection development : the selection of materials for libraries. " New York: Holt, 1980.

Katz, William A. "Collection development : the selection of materials for libraries." New York, Holt, Rinehart and Winston 1980.

Kee, W.A. "Availability of technical reports." *Sci-Tech News* 16(1) Spring 1962: 7-9.

Kennedy, Gail A. "The relationship between acquisitions and collection development." *Library Acquisitions: Practice and Theory* 7(3) 1983: 225-232.

Kent, Allen, et al. *Use of library materials: The University of Pittsburgh.* New York: Marcel Dekker Inc., 1979.

Kent, Allen and Lancour, Harold ed. *Encyclopedia of library and information science* New York: Marcel Dekker, 1980. Vol. 30.

Klempner, I.M. "The concept of national security and its effect on information transfer." *Special Libraries* 64 (7) July 1973: 263-269.

Knox, William T. "Special libraries and NTIS." *Special Libraries* (1) January 1976: 45-48.

Kohl, David F. "Collection Development : an overview of the research." *Collection Management* 10(3/4) 1988: 1-13.

Kraft, Donald H. and Polacsek, Richard, A. "A journal worth measure for a journal selection decision model." *Collection Management* 2(2) Summer 1978: 129-139.

Lane, Alfred H. *Gifts and exchange manual* London: Aldwych Press, 80.

Lazzell, R.E. *Points of contact: scientific and technical information.* AD-746615. Arlington VA: US Army R&D Information System Office, 1972.

Leimicuhler, Ferdinand F. Evaluation of costs and benefits of libraries. Arlington, VA, ERIC Document Reproduction Service, 1978. ERIC-Report-ED-163947. (A paper presented at the Annual Conference of the Special Libraries Association, Kansas City, Missouri, June 1978).

Lin, Nan and Garvey, William D. "Information needs and uses." In Carlos A. Cuadra ed. *Annual Review of Information Science and Technology.* Chicago: Encyclopaedia Britannica Inc., 1972. Vol. 7: 5-37.

Loertscher, David V. "Collection mapping : An evaluation strategy for collection development." *Drexel Library Quarterly* 21(2) Spring 1985: 9-21.

Lungberg, Sixton et al. "Investigation on the use of information in R&D at a research intensive company, Phase II: Possibilities of economic evaluation." *Tidsk Dokum* 32(2) 1976: 17-23.

Maass, Barbara. "The new mythology : cooperative collection development." Canadian Library Journal 46(1) Feb. 1989: 23-29.

Macadam, E.J. "Locating technical reports from USA." *Aircraft Engineering* 45(5) May 1973: 49-50.

Magrill, Rose Mary and Hickey, Doralyn J. *Acquisitions management and collection development in libraries*. Chicago: ALA, 1984.

Mangla, P.B. ed. "Building library collections and national policy for library and information services." Delhi: Indian Library Association, 1985.

Mazal, Otto. "The acquisition policy of special subject collections of one library." *LIBER Bulletin* 30 1988: 61-67.

Mc Clung, A. ed. Selection of library materials in the humanities, social sciences and sciences, Chicago: ALA, 1985.

McGarry, Kevin. *Communication, Knowledge and the Librarian* London: Clive Bingley, 1975.

Miller, Ruth H. and Niemeicer, Martha, W. "Vendor performance : A study of two libraries. Library Resources and Technical Services. January-March 1987: 60-68.

Moore, L. et al. Distinction is all-NTIS from a technical librarian's point-of-view. ED-050913. Washington: US Office of Education, 1971.

Morton, Bruce, "Toward a comprehensive collection development policy for partial U.S. depository libraries." *Government Publications Review* 7A(1) 1980: 41-46.

Mosher, Paul H. "Collection development to collection management : toward stewardship of library resources." *Collection Management* 4(4) Winter 1982: 41-48.

Mosher, Paul H. and Pankake, Marcia. "A guide to coordinated and cooperative collection development." *Library Resources and Technical Services* 27(4). October-December 1983: 420.

Murray, William et al. "Collection mapping and collection development." *Drexel Library Quarterly* 21(2) Spring 1985: 40-51.

NASA, STIO. The NASA information system. . . and how to use it. NASA, n.d.

National Academy of Science and National Academy of Engineering and Committee on Scientific and Technical Communication. "Scientific and technical communication: A pressing national problem and recommendations for its solution" Washington DC: National Academy of Sciences, 1969 116.

Nazim, Ali S. "Acquisition of scientific literature in developing countries." *Information Development* 5(2) April 1989: 73-115.

Nelson, Carl E. *Microfilm Technology : Engineering and Related Fields,* New York: McGraw-Hill book, 1965.

Nientimp, Judith A. "The Librarian . . .[and the subscription agent]." Special Libraries July 1972: 291-292, 295-297.

Nisonger, Thomas E. "Report on the AMIGOS workshop: Acquisitions and collection development : Cooperation in a changing environment." *Library Acquisitions: Practice and Theory* 12(1) 1988: 73-77.

NMA. "How to select a microform reader or a reader printer" Maryland: NMA, 1974.

———. "The user's guide to standard microfiche formats" Maryland: NMA, 1976.

Null, David G. "Robbing peter . . . balancing collection development and reference responsibilities." *College and Research Libraries* 49(5) September 1988: 448-452.

Nyren, Karl ed. *Collections Development.* New York, R.R. Bowker Company, Xerox Publishing Division 1978.

Oldman, Christine. "Value of Information" Library Research Occasional Paper No.1. Bradford. MCB Publications, 1976.

Olson, Lowell E. "Blind spots in collection development." Top of the News 41(4) Summer 1985: 371-376.

Osburn, Charles B. "Non-use and loser studies in collection development" Collection Management 4(1/2) Spring/Summer 1982: 45-53.

———. "Toward a reconceptualisation of collection development." In: G. McCabe and B. Kreissman ed. Advances in library administration and organisation vol. 2 London: Jai Press 1983: 175-198.

Pankake, Marcia. "From book selection to collection management : continuity and advance in an unending work." In: Wesley Simonton ed. Advances in Librarianship. V.13. Orlando: Academic Press, 1984: 185-210.

Paterson, Brian, "Breathe new life into your collection." Cape Librarian 31(4) April 1987: 5-7.

Perkins, David L. Guidelines for collection development. Chicago: ALA, 1979.

Perkins, David L. "Writing the collection development manual." Collection Management 4(3) Fall 1982: 37-47.

———. "Writing the collection development manual." *Collection Building* 4(3) Fall 1982: 37-47.

Perdue, Albert. "Conflicts in collection development." *Library Acquisitions: Practice and Theory* 2(2) 1978: 123-126.

Pilling, Stella. "Collection development : options for effective management." *UK Serials Group Newsletter* 9(2) December 1987: 39-40.

Rafeel, Jeffrey. "From economic to political analysis of library decision-making." *College and Research Libraries* 35(6) Nov. 1974: 412-423.

Raitt, David Iain. Communication and Information Seeking and Use Habits of Scientists and Engineers in International Organisations and National Aerospace Research Establishments in Europe. Ph.D. Thesis. Loughborough: Loughborough University of Technology, 1984.

Rawdin, Eugene. "Field survey of information needs of industry sci/tech library users." In *Proceedings* of the 38th ASIS Annual Meeting. New York: Greenwood, 1975: 12, 41-42.

Redman, Helen F. "Report number chaos." *Special Libraries* 53(10) December 1962: 574-578.

Richardson, Wiliam H. "Report numbers : boon or bugaboo?" *Sci-Tech News* 15(1) Spring 1961: 5-6, 9.

Roberto, Elizabeth P. "Cooperative collection development of science serials." *Serials Librarian* 14(1/2) 1988: 19-31.

Robertson, S.E. and Hansman, Sandy. "Journal acquisition by libraries : scatter and cost effectiveness." *Journal of Documentation* 31(4) Dec. 1979: 273-282.

Root, Nina J. "Decision-making for collection management." *Collection Management* 7(1) Spring 1985: 93-101.

Rutledge, John and Swindler, Luke, "The selection decision : defining criteria and establishing priorities." *College and Research Libraries* 48(2) March 1987: 123-131. Stam, David H. "Collaborative collection development : progress, problems and potential." *Collection Building* 7(3) 1986: 3-8.

Sargent, Charles W. "Handling technical reports in the medical library." *Bulletin of Medical Library Association* 57(1) January 1969: 41-46.

Shubert, Joseph F. "Coordinated collection development for the purpose of resource sharing." *Collection Management* 7(1) Spring 1985: 75-83.

Shuchman, Hedvah L. Information Transfer in Engineering. Rep-461-46-27. Connecticut; Futures Group Inc., 1981.

———. "Information technology and the technologist : A report on a national study of American engineers." *International Forum on Information and Documentation* 7(1) January 1982. 3-8.

Silvo, Manil. "Special Libraries" London: Andre Deutsch, 1970.

Singh, B.N. "Information needs of engineering scientists." *International Library Review* 13(2) April 1981: 167-188.

Slater, Margaret and Fisher, P. *Use Made of Technical Libraries*, Aslib Occasional Publication No. 2. London: Aslib, 1969.

Smethurst, J.M. "Resource sharing and conspectus in the British Library." *Liber News Sheet* (21) 1987: 26-30.

Sohn, Jeanne, "Collection development organisational patterns in ARL libraries." *Library Resources and Technical Services* 31(2) April/June 1987: 123-134.

Sowell, Steven L. "Expanding horizons in collection development with expert systems : development and testing of a demonstration prototype." *Special Libraries* 1980 (1) 1989: 45-50.

Spiller, David. "Book selection : an introduction to principles and practice" 3 ed. New York: K.G. Saur, 1980.

Sridhar, M.S. "Prospects and problems of microforms in libraries." *Journal of Library and Information Science* 6(2) December 1981: 1-15.

———. "Role of report in scientific and technical information transfer." *IASLIC Bulletin* 27(2) June 1982: 99-104.

———. "User participation in collection building in a special library : a case study." *IASLIC Bulletin* 28(3) September 1983: 99-106.

———. "Hazards of report numbers." In: Information Flow in Non-R&D Context and Grey Literature: Papers Presented at XIV IASLIC Conference, 26-29 December 1983, New Delhi ed. by A.R. Chakraborty and S.K. Kapoor. Calcutta: IASLIC, 1983: 139-142.

———. "Problems and choices in procurement of technical reports." *Library Science with a Slant to Documentation* 20(2) June 1983: 107-124.

———. "Use of technical reports and standards." *IASLIC Bulletin* 29(3) September 1984: 99-106.

———. "Are demand forecasting techniques applicable to libraries?" Library Herald 23 July-October 1984: 84-89.

———. "Book procurement delay : a demotivator to user participation in collection development." In Building Library Collections and National Policy for Library and Information Services: Seminar Papers of 30th All India Library Conference, Rajasthan University, Jaipur, 28-31 January 1985. Delhi: ILA, 1985: 329-334.

———. "A decision theory approach to standing order procurement of NASA reports." *Annals of Library Science and Documentation* 32(1-2) March-June 1985: 15-22.

———. "Ratio analysis technique : a tool for assessing the health of a library." In: Financial Management of Library and Information Centres: Papers Presented at XII IASLIC National Seminar 1986, Banaras Hindu University, Varanasi, 18-31 December 1986: Calcutta: IASLIC 1986: 137-146.

———. "Use of current journals by Indian space technologists." *The Serials Librarian* 10(3) Spring 1986: 77-93.

———. "Problems of document acquisition in science and technology libraries." In: *Proceedings* of the workshop on collection development of libraries and use of engineering literature in science and technology institutions, 15-18 January 1986, Karnataka Regional Engineering College, Surathkal. Surathkal: Karnataka Regional Engineering College, 1986: 5.7.1-5.7.11.

INDEX

CICIL LIST

CONCEPTS IN COMMUNICATION, INFORMATICS & LIBRARIANSHIP

(CICIL)

General Editor: **S.P. AGRAWAL**

CICIL-1 Development of Library Services in India: Social Science Information
S.P. Agrawal Rs. 150

CICIL-2 Development of Documentation in India: Social Science Information
S.P. Agrawal Rs. 250

CICIL-3 UNESCO and Social Sciences: Retrospect and Prospect
S.P. Agrawal and **J.C. Aggarwal** Rs. 250

CICIL-4 INDIANA : A Bibliography of Bibliographical Sources
M.K. Jain Rs. 200

CICIL-5 Dimensions of Library and Information Science: Kaula Festschrift
V. Venkatappaiah (Eds.) Rs. 600

CICIL-6 Book Numbers: Some Indian Methods
M.P. Satija and **S.P. Agrawal** Rs. 100

CICIL-7 National Policy for University Libraries in India: Problems and Perspectives
N.B. Inamdar and **L.S. Ramaiah** (Ed.) Rs. 250

CICIL-8 Media Utilisation for the Development of Women and Children
B.S. Thakur and **Binod C. Agrawal** Rs. 150

CICIL-9 Terrorism: An Annotated Bibliography
Susheela Bhan (Ed.) Rs. 275

CICIL-10 Transnational Library Relations: The Indo-American Experience
M.B. Konnur Rs. 175

CICIL-11 Geography of Marketing and Commercial Activities in India (Documentation on Research Information)
R.S. Dixit Rs. 130

CICIL-12 Information India 1988: Global View
S.P. Agrawal and **J.C. Aggarwal** Rs. 200

CICIL-13 Women's Education in India: Historical Review, Present Status and Perspective Plan
S.P. Agrawal and **J.C. Aggarwal** Rs. 360

CICIL-14 Cultural Communication in India: Role and Impact of Phonograms
J.M. Ojha (in press)

CICIL-15 Second Historical Survey of Educational Development in India: Select Documents 1985-1989
S.P. Agrawal and **J.C. Aggarwal** Rs. 490

CICIL-16 Documentation Encyclopaedia of UNESCO and Education
J.C. Aggarwal and **S.P. Agrawal** Rs. 800 (set of 2 parts)

CICIL-17 Attitude Towards Information: A Study of Post-Graduate Teachers and Researchers in Social Sciences
N.G. Satish (in press)

CICIL-18 Librarianship and Bureaucratic Organisation: A Study in the Sociology of Library Profession in India
P.K. Jayaswal Rs. 175

CICIL-19 Literature Search
K.A. Isaac Rs. 150

CICIL-20 Child Education in India: Index to Scholarly Writings in Indian Educational Journals and Newspapers since independence
S.P. Agrawal and **Naresh Kanta** Rs. 100

CICIL-21 Lok Sabha and Vidhan Sabha Elections in India 1989 & 1990: Process and Results with Comparative Study of Manifestos
S.P. Agrawal and **J.C. Aggarwal** Rs. 250

CICIL-22 Islamic Studies in India: A Survey of Human, Institutional and Documentary Sources
Mohamed Taher Rs. 180

CICIL-23 Panchayati Raj: An Annotated Bibliography
N.B. Inamdar, N.G. Satish and **Anil Takalkar** 290

CICIL-24 Information India 1989-90: Global View
S.P. Agrawal and **J.C. Aggarwal** Rs. 500